INTRODUCTION TO
SOCIAL RESEARCH

57¢ TRA

INTRODUCTION TO SOCIAL RESEARCH

Second Edition

Sanford Labovitz
University of Calgary, Canada

Robert Hagedorn
University of Victoria, Canada

McGraw-Hill Book Company

New York   St. Louis   San Francisco   Auckland   Düsseldorf
Johannesburg   Kuala Lumpur   London   Mexico   Montreal
New Delhi   Panama   Paris   São Paulo   Singapore
Sydney   Tokyo   Toronto

Library of Congress Cataloging in Publication Data

Labovitz, Sanford, date
    Introduction to social research.

    Includes bibliographies and index.
    1.   Social science research.   I.   Hagedorn, Robert,
date joint author.   II.   Title.
H62.L24 1975   300′.7′2   75-6909
ISBN 0-07-035776-5
ISBN 0-07-035775-7 pbk.

INTRODUCTION TO SOCIAL RESEARCH

234567890MUMU79876

This book was set in Times Roman by Black Dot, Inc.
The editors were Lyle Linder and Phyllis T. Dulan;
the cover was designed by Pencils Portfolio, Inc.;
the production supervisor was Charles Hess.
The Murray Printing Company was printer and binder.

for un ojo and the gibber

Contents

5

Methods of Observation   *71*

6

Data Analysis   *88*

7

Decision Making in Scientific Research   *114*

Preface

All too frequently, students leave introductory social science courses without having gained an understanding of the research process or the ability to interpret the research findings presented in their text. The major goal of this book is to change this situation by introducing the student to a basic understanding of social research. Preliminary usage of this book in introductory classes indicates that students can understand the material with little or no explanation by the instructor. The book is self-explanatory, which permits the instructor either to elaborate on certain aspects of social research or to emphasize substantive material in class. Although the book is oriented primarily to undergraduate students in social science courses, including introductory and social research, it may serve as a review for graduate students.

The debts incurred in writing this book are monumental. Many of the ideas, as well as the clarity of presentation, can be attributed to our teachers, colleagues, and students. Nevertheless, there are always a few who are directly involved in the process of completing a book. In particular, Vern Bengtson and Michael Mend were extremely helpful in sharing their ideas with us. We would like to thank them, along with Judy Friedman, Bartolomeo Palisi, and Clarence Tygart, for their constructive criticisms of an earlier draft. Finally, special thanks should go to Elizabeth Hagedorn, Vikki Labovitz, John McComb, and Jon Miller for their comments on specific chapters and problems. All these individuals not only improved the quality of the book, but frequently saved us from embarrassment.

Sanford Labovitz
Robert Hagedorn

Chapter 1

Evidence and Causal Analysis

The major goal of scientific research is to establish causal laws that enable us to predict and explain specific phenomena. At a minimum, to establish these laws a science must have reliable and valid information or facts. To obtain reliable and valid facts it is mandatory to follow explicit rules to determine the degree of relative truth of any item of information. Ascertaining the exact nature of a "fact," however, and deciding just what determines whether a bit of information is a fact are extremely complex problems.

College students are inundated with facts. They are fed chemical facts, historical facts, physical facts, psychological facts, and social facts. Sometimes they even question the facts; that is, they do not think that whatever is presented to them is necessarily a fact. Stated otherwise, they do not unquestioningly accept a statement as true.

Just what is a fact? A fact is a reliable and valid item of information. It could be a behavior (the group voted for their president to serve another term), an attitude (the veterans are against amnesty to deserters), a law (people of different races in the Union of South Africa cannot intermarry), or even a statistic (the suicide rate for Canada in 1972 was 11.0). It is important for the information to be reliable, that is, that repeated observations of the same phenomenon yield similar results (see the discussion of reliability in Chapter 2); and that the observations actually yield measures of what they are supposed to measure (validity). A theory is not a fact, and a hypothesis is not a fact. A fact is not a proposed relationship or condition. A fact is a well-documented item of information.

What, therefore, is the basis for accepting or rejecting something as a fact? This is the central question of scientific research, and it is crucial to decision and policy making in, for example, business and government. How do we come by facts or reliable and valid information?

the nature of evidence

Among the lay public (nonscientists), there are three common bases for establishing facts: (1) authority (a teacher, parent, or expert says it is so, and you accept it); (2) intuition (you just know it is so, such as when you believe in the existence of a god or believe in the superiority of a particular approach to raising children); and (3) logic (it follows according to specified rules). Because each of these criteria can lead to false conclusions, scientists have found it necessary to develop their own criteria for establishing facts (and establishing valid relations between facts). These criteria are labeled *the scientific method.*

To make a comparison with establishing facts by the

scientific method (based on observation), consider a religious argument for "proving" the existence of God. An analogy is made between the complex mechanisms of a watch and the complex, intricate patterns of the universe. Based on the notion that it took a highly intelligent mind to design the watch, it is concluded that it must have taken a supreme, all-knowing being to design the universe, which is vastly more complex. The validity of this argument is not based on the careful observation of a supreme being, but on a logical argument involving an analogy (the universe and a watch) and an inference (the universe is infinitely more complex than is a watch, and therefore, its design required a superior mind).

Such statements as "women belong in the home," "Jews are money-hungry," "the French are great lovers," "dolphins are as intelligent as humans," and "people are basically evil" or even "people are basically good" cannot be treated as scientific facts. They may or may not be true, but they are based on some form of intuition or nonfactual stereotyping. They cannot be considered reliable items of information.

In sharp contrast to the existence of God analogy and to intuitive statements, scientific information is based on reliable and valid observation. The remainder of this book can be viewed as a presentation of the scientific method for validating sociological facts and cause-and-effect relations between such facts. In this sense, the scientific method is a way of thinking and problem solving; it is an orientation to the empirical world; and it is the technique most sociologists use to build a science of social phenomena.

the nature of causality

Cause, in one way or another, is central to the goal of establishing scientific laws. In general terms, causation refers to the factors that make designated phenomena happen or change. To illustrate, a specific virus or organism causes malaria, and long periods of drinking may produce cirrhosis of the liver. In the social sciences, the precise causes of events are not unequivocally established. Although there are many citizens who think that one of the causes leading to the use of LSD, heroin, or morphine is the smoking of marijuana, this is far from proved. There are persons who have gone the route from marijuana to the more "serious" drugs; however, many "pot" smokers do not use other drugs, and some users of the more serious drugs have not smoked pot. This information clearly calls into question the suggested causal sequence stipulating that persons go from using marijuana to using other drugs. This sequence is usually justified on the grounds that pot smokers eventually want or need increasingly greater "kicks." Even if all users of the more serious drugs started with pot smoking, we could not unequivocally say that one led to the other. Almost all drug users started out with milk, and we would hardly label such consumption as a cause of, say, heroin addiction. Drug usage seems to be an extremely complex behavior pattern and is not caused exclusively by such single factors as the need for greater kicks or even by a physical dependency.

There are at least four widely accepted scientific criteria for establishing causality. These criteria are *association, time priority, nonspurious relation,* and *rationale.*

MAGNITUDE AND CONSISTENCY OF ASSOCIATION   It is widely accepted that if two or more variables are not associated, one cannot be the cause of the other. For example, eye color is not considered a cause of height, nor is marital status considered a cause of intelligence. These two sets of variables are assumed to be nonrelated, although some small statistical relation may exist between them.

An association is a necessary condition for a causal relation. If education is not related to popularity, it cannot be the cause of popularity. Consider the plausible ideas that maternal deprivation leads to delinquency and low intelligence leads to crime. A lack of an association between the variables in these two hypotheses would require the rejection of any causal connection. That is, if nondeprived youths are just as likely to be delinquent as those who are deprived, maternal deprivation is not a cause of delinquency. Similarly, if persons with low and high IQs are just as likely to commit crimes, intelligence is not a cause of criminality.

There are two characteristics of an association that generally strengthen the conclusion that one variable is at least a partial cause of the other. The first is *magnitude,* which refers to the size or strength of the association. (See the chapter on descriptive statistics.) For example, smokers have a rate of lung cancer that is about eleven times greater than among nonsmokers. Although not a sufficient condition for establishing causation, the greater the magnitude of the association between smoking and lung cancer, the more confidence one has that the relation is truly causal. High magnitude alone, however, definitely is not a sufficient condition for a causal interpretation. The high positive relation between the number of fire engines and the amount of fire damage (the more fire engines present, the more the damage) is well documented. Fires, however, not the fire engines, come first; and firemen put fires out (usually) rather than increasing them. We cannot say, therefore, that the presence of many fire engines causes severe fire damage.

Consider the two hypothetical situations in Table 1 as an illustration of the extremes in magnitude of association. In situation 1 there is a very high association (high magnitude) between the social classes of father and son. All sons with upper-class fathers are upper-class; all with middle-class fathers are middle-class; and all with lower-class fathers are lower-class. The magnitude of the association in situation 2 is not nearly as high. Although there is some tendency for sons to have the same social class as their fathers (witness the larger numbers in the main diagonal cells), there are a large number of sons with social classes different from their fathers'. The first situation probably characterizes a rigid class structure (as exists among the castes of India), while the second probably characterizes a relatively free or changing class structure (as may to some extent characterize the United States and Australia).

The second characteristic of an association that increas-

TABLE 1. *Extremes in magnitude of association*

SITUATION 1				SITUATION 2			
Social Class of Father	Social Class of Son			Social Class of Father	Social Class of Son		
	Upper	Middle	Lower		Upper	Middle	Lower
Upper	60	0	0	Upper	25	20	15
Middle	0	60	0	Middle	20	25	15
Lower	0	0	60	Lower	15	20	25

es the plausibility of a causal interpretation is *consistency.* If the relation persists from one study to the next under a variety of conditions, confidence in the causal nature of the relation is increased. For example, one of the major arguments supporting the notion that certain types of cancer are caused by smoking is that the relation between smoking and cancer is maintained in study after study. The relation exists (1) in prospective studies (e.g., the smoking habits of people are studied to see who develops cancer) as well as in retrospective studies (e.g., old hospital records are checked); (2) in different localities, such as countries, regions within a country, and rural and urban areas; (3) in studies of rats as well as in studies of people; (4) among different ethnic and racial groups; (5) among females as well as males; and (6) from one time period to another.

The magnitude of an association should be treated only as a guide in assessing causality. A true causal association, for example, may exist when two variables are just barely related because there may be several factors producing an event. All the factors may be important because they combine their small influences to cause an event. For example, possible causal factors in individuals' decisions to join organizations may include leadership abilities, education, power seeking, and attempting to establish business contacts. All of these factors may be necessary to explain organizational membership.

The consistency of association also should be considered cautiously. All scientific laws are conditional; that is, they apply only under certain circumstances. For example, the law of gravity is stated in terms of a perfect vacuum. At one time the relation between smoking and cancer was considered by some to be causal only for males. Consequently, if results are not consistent, it may be that the causal relation is valid only in certain situations.

TIME PRIORITY To establish cause, the independent causal variable must either occur first or change prior to the dependent variable. The independent variable is the causal factor that produces the effect or dependent variable. Smoking is considered by many to be the independent variable that causes lung cancer (the dependent variable). The time-priority assumption is based on the "common-sense" notion that an event in the future cannot determine an event in the past or present.

There are many relations where it is fairly easy to establish the time priority among variables. For example, among females, physical maturation occurs prior to the ability to conceive; formal education usually occurs prior to marital happiness (or unhappiness); smoking in an overwhelmingly high percentage of cases begins before the person develops cancer, rather than cancer victims picking up the smoking habit; and severity of parental supervision starts long before success in college.

There are, however, many relations where time priority is difficult to determine. Although technology and urbanization are related (technologically advanced countries tend to be highly urbanized), it is far from established whether technology changes prior to changes in urbanization, or vice versa. Do we first look at an advertisement and then buy the product, or do we buy the product and then search out the advertisement? Do individuals of high socioeconomic status participate in community organizations as a result of their status, or do they get high status from extensive community participation?

Whether it is difficult or easy to establish a time priority among variables depends to some extent on the *logic* of the situation, on *observation,* on *theory,* and on *data analysis.* The logic of the situation is generally established by rejecting the reverse temporal sequence. A child must first develop and strengthen his sphincter muscles before he can be toilet trained, rather than the reverse sequence. Clearly, a child must be able to exert some muscular control before he can be trained. The same logic applies to the sequence implied in the saying that a child must crawl before he can walk. That is, certain logical requirements set up the time priority.

The technique of observation indicates that through our sense perceptions we can determine time priority. For example, we may observe that people smoke for many years, and then some develop cancer; or we observe that individuals first go to college, and then they enter certain high-prestige occupations. In experiments, time priority is relatively easy to determine. For example, if we administer a speed-reading course to a group of college students and then compute their grade-point average for the following year, it is clear that the experimental variable (speed-reading course) occurred prior to the recorded college performance.

The third technique for establishing causal priority is theory. According to a rationale involving clearly spelled-out assumptions, the time priority of certain variables is hypothesized. Consider the example of technology and urbanization. Suppose it is assumed that persons must first physically locate themselves close to one another before some can spend time inventing and experimenting. Another assumption may be that a certain amount of time must be spent inventing and experimenting before an area can change from a simple to a complex technological base. Although these assumptions may be wrong, they lead to the conclusion that urbanization occurs prior to technological innovation.

Finally, analysis of the associations between two variables over a period of time by *cross-lagging* may suggest the appropriate time priority. The cross-lagging technique compares two associations between two variables by first taking the initial values of one variable (IQ scores of students in 1968) and pairing them off with the values of another variable at a later time period (grade-point averages, or GPAs, in 1970). Second, the time sequence is reversed for the variables; for example, the students' GPAs in 1968 are paired off with their IQ scores in 1970. The initial variable in the situation that shows the highest association is assumed to have changed first or to have occurred prior in time. To illustrate, if IQ scores in 1968 are more closely related to GPAs in 1970 than vice versa (GPAs in 1968 and IQ scores in 1970), then IQ is assumed to have changed first.

Although time priority is almost universally considered a necessary condition for causality, many scientists will accept causal interpretations if the variables in question change or happen simultaneously, rather than one occurring before the other.

NONSPURIOUS RELATION   A nonspurious relation is defined as an association between two variables that cannot be explained by a third variable. Stated otherwise, if the effects of all relevant variables are eliminated and the relation between the independent and dependent variables is maintained, then the relation is nonspurious. (See the discussion of control variables in the section on multivariate statistics.) For example, if the relation between smoking and cancer (i.e., smokers develop cancer at a rate eleven times greater than do nonsmokers) is unaffected when computed separately for males and females (or for rural and urban residents or for heavy, medium, and light body builds), then the relation is not a false one. That is, if it is shown that men who smoke have a higher rate of cancer than nonsmoking men and women smokers have a higher rate of cancer than nonsmoking women, then the smoking and cancer relation is not explained by sex differences.

Table 2 demonstrates this hypothetical nonspurious relation between smoking and cancer given the differences between men and women. The original table based on both men

TABLE 2. *Hypothetical example of a nonspurious relation between smoking and cancer because of sex differences*

MEN AND WOMEN COMBINED

	Lung Cancer	
Smoke	Yes	No
Yes	100	0
No	0	100

MEN ONLY				WOMEN ONLY		
	Lung Cancer				Lung Cancer	
Smoke	Yes	No		Smoke	Yes	No
Yes	50	0		Yes	50	0
No	0	50		No	0	50

and women is separated into two tables—one for men and the other for women. The close high-magnitude relation between smoking and cancer in the combined table still exists for men alone and for women alone.

Assuming that the effects of all relevant variables have been eliminated, then we can be more confident in interpreting the relation as being causal and not due to other factors. If it can be shown, however, that certain genetic factors both predispose a person to smoking and determine who will develop lung cancer, then it would be spurious to interpret the relation between smoking and cancer as causal.

Consider, now, the spurious causal interpretation of the correlation between the number of fire engines involved in a fire and the amount of fire damage. Clearly it is wrong to interpret the relation as indicating that fire engines cause the damage. If we controlled on the severity of the fire (in terms of extent, duration, and amount of heat generated), we would find that when fires are not severe few fire engines are involved and the amount of fire damage is minimal. With severe fires, however, a large number of fire engines are called and damage is extensive.

In this case, the causal interpretation of the relation between fire engines and damage is spurious because it can be explained by the severity of the fire.

Controlling for all relevant variables is the basic problem in trying to determine whether or not the interpretation of a relation is spurious. As we will discuss in the chapter on design, only in experiments and through a process called *randomization* is it possible to control for all other factors (both known and unknown). In most designs used by sociologists, randomization is not possible, and selection of control variables must be determined by the researcher. In nonexperimental designs, usually only a few variables can be selected for control. Consequently, some relevant variables may not be controlled, and the spuriousness of the relation cannot be assessed.

There are three rough guides for the researcher when he is limited to controlling on a few select variables. First, a time priority should be determined for the third variable, because to explain a relationship a variable must occur prior in time to both independent and dependent variables. Second, theory may help determine the relevance of the control variables. Theory suggests which control variables may be relevant by indicating how they may affect the original relation. Finally, previous empirical research is an important guide to selecting variables. Research findings give some indication of how and to what extent the independent and dependent variables have been influenced by selected potential control variables.

RATIONALE   The rationale refers to the theory, explanation, or interpretation of a relation stipulating that not only does the independent variable change first, but it also causes changes in the dependent variable. The rationale is the justification for the observed relation, which is often stated in terms of assumptions and hypotheses. For example, it has been shown that a lack of status integration (persons occupying positions that make conflicting demands and expectations) leads to higher suicide rates. A rationale to interpret the relation as causal is that conflicting demands and expectations lead to emotional stress, which, in turn, leads to suicide.

A rationale may specify the causal nature of a relation by designating the *intervening mechanisms* that connect the independent and dependent variables. Consider the relation between broken homes and delinquency. To justify the interpretation that broken homes lead to delinquency, it may be hypothesized that broken homes are characterized by a lack of supervision which ultimately leads to delinquency. One major argument presented by spokesmen for the tobacco industry against the causal interpretation of smoking and lung cancer centers around the intervening mechanism. This argument, in essence, suggests that the agent or mechanism that results from smoking and produces cancer has not been isolated (if, indeed, such an agent exists at all). It has not been established that certain tars or carcinogens from cigarettes produce cancerous cells. If, however, such an agent is found, the wind would be taken out of the arguments suggesting that the relation between smoking and cancer is statistical rather than causal.

Another case illustrating the importance of a rationale is the relation between occupational prestige and participation in community organizations. It may be argued that persons enter prestigious occupations and then participate in the affairs of the community. Even if this time sequence is well documented, it may be spurious to conclude that occupational prestige is the cause of participation. A third variable may not only predispose an individual to a prestigious occupation, but it may also predispose him to participating in community organizations. Formal education (college versus noncollege graduates) is a plausible variable for explaining the relation between occupational prestige and community participation. Not only do most prestigious occupations (physicians, lawyers, physicists, etc.) require a high educational level, but a college education instills attitudes, skills, and knowledge that are conducive to participation (for example, knowledge of the existence of community organizations and how to join them, awareness of community problems, and skills for coordinating activities and working with others).

TWO LESS ACCEPTED FACTORS CONCERNING CAUSES   All scientists are concerned with ordering their worlds of interest, and the four causal criteria represent one way of doing this. There are, however, at least two other ways of establishing order in the world that are deemed important by selected groups of social scientists. Although there are many who oppose these ways (and some violently), they are briefly presented to give some indication of the complexity of thought about causality. These factors are *purpose* and *empathy* (or understanding). Those who espouse purpose or empathy usually follow the general scientific approach to some extent, but they apparently feel that this approach is too limited (by itself) for analyzing social phenomena.

Purpose is a notion (often associated with an approach in sociology called *functionalism*) that specifies that an event is explained if we can determine the purpose it serves for the group or society. The rain dance among the Hopi Indians can be explained if we recognize that it serves the purpose of promoting solidarity in the group. As another case, the system of law enforcement in a society can be explained by its purpose of keeping the society together.

There are two related problems stemming from the use of purpose as a factor in establishing causation. First, to establish the purpose of an event, a scientist often waits until it has occurred; but to wait until the event has occurred appears to be placing the causal variable (the event) after the fact (the effect). This, on the surface at least, violates the time-priority criterion for establishing cause. We must wait for the Hopi rain dance to occur before we can say that it promotes group solidarity. A second ramification is that purpose appears to be based on some notion of meeting societal needs to maintain a "normal" state. For example, for a normal Hopi society, group solidarity (a societal need) must be promoted.

Besides the apparent contradiction in time priority, the needs of society and the meaning of a normal state have not been clearly established. Consequently, purpose is a difficult notion to apply. Some scientists, however, feel it is crucial to establish both the cause and the function of social phenomena.

Empathy, or understanding (often associated with an approach in sociology called *Verstehen*), is a type of causal explanation that stresses a similarity in emotional feeling between the scientist and the actor (subject). To explain why a person committed suicide, we try to place ourselves in his place (take the role of the other) and experience what he experienced. By emotionally experiencing his reaction to the death of his wife (an abrupt retirement because of injury, his child's terminal illness, or imminent bankruptcy), we can get an indication of how the victim felt before his suicide.

An empathetic "explanation" is based on the satisfaction a scientist has with his interpretation of an event. This satisfaction may accrue if he can summarize briefly "the guts of a phenomenon"; for example, rape may be explained as a response to sexual frustration. Those who accept the empathetic orientation want to go beyond the establishment of the causes of social phenomena to the point where these phenomena are "understood." That is, an adequate rationale that leads to a high level of prediction is not enough for these social scientists. They must also understand. This understanding is based on some personal judgment, or feeling, and may be summed up best by the statement, "I know how you feel."

problems in causal analysis

Determining the causes of social events has proved to be a difficult task. It takes a vast amount of research and theoretical development before reliable and valid statements can be made concerning association, time priority, nonspuriousness, and rationale.

There is a general consensus that the development of

any science requires both a solid base of investigation and a body of statements regarding the nature of relationships. Science, therefore, requires both research and theory; these two basic factors are intimately related. A scientist is not likely to carry out meaningful research without the guidance of a relevant and clearly stated theory, and a scientist is not likely to develop a relevant and clearly stated theory without the guidance of reliable research findings.

We are not stressing the importance of theory over research or of research over theory. A science gradually develops in a dialectic process involving continuous shifts back and forth between research and theory. Theory guides the researcher into important problems, it specifies the significant variables of investigation, and it suggests ways these variables can be measured and interrelated. Research provides tests for the validity of a theory, and its findings can suggest ways of modifying a theory. By scientists' working back and forth between research and theory (investigations and ideas), theory should become more refined and valid, and research should become more specific and relevant for testing.

Impressions of the social order or facts about society are incomprehensible in isolation. They must be given meanings by a theory. That one person is a manager and another is a laborer is meaningless until we specify the implications of such occupations. Based on a large number of observations and on theory, the implications are diverse and of extreme importance. Managers, as compared to laborers, have, for example, more power and influence in decision making, a different and "better" life-style, more material goods, and a different and "better" reward system. They are more educated and belong to more community organizations. Meaning is given to occupational differences by stating the relations of occupation to important social factors (power, rewards, life-style, education, and organizational membership). Statements on the nature of the relations are a major part of the theory.

Theories have a profound effect on social research. Suppose it is assumed that one's work has a major influence over interpersonal relations both on and off the job. It may be argued that work is a dominant force in one's life because of several factors: (1) a large amount of time is put into it; (2) it bestows recognition on the individual (he or she is a professor, or a race driver, or a bus driver); (3) it bestows prestige on the individual; (4) it shapes individual attitudes and beliefs (managers are more likely to favor an incentive-reward system while workers are more likely to favor a seniority system); and (5) it provides an income which largely determines the quantity and quality of acquired goods, the nature and length of vacations, the length and type of education for children, and the adequacy and extent of medical care (among many others). Because of these factors, which form the bases for a theory, research into work has been extensive. The theory, furthermore, guides the scientist by specifying where the effects of the work situation probably will be manifest—in this illustration in recognition, prestige, attitudes, beliefs, and life-style.

The above is only a rudimentary sketch of the possible interrelations between theory and research. The process can take many forms and can be extremely complex. At times research may be overemphasized to the detriment of theory development ("hard nosed" researchers who just "want the facts"); at other times theory may be overemphasized to the detriment of research ("armchair" theory builders who do not want to be bothered with the facts). It is unfortunate for science to separate the researcher from the theorist. For the development of a science they must be inseparable and based on a feedback connection going both ways from theory to research and from research to theory.

There are some critical problems in the interplay between theory and research concerned with social phenomena. These problems impede the process of establishing the causes of events and include (1) the complexity of social causation and (2) the potential biases and limitations in studying human behavior.

THE COMPLEXITY OF SOCIAL CAUSATION   Any particular social event may have several determinants. The causes of a suicide may include a loss of a loved one, a loss of status, access to barbiturates or a gun, a change in marital status, and a business loss. All these factors may be operating, and others of an unknown nature may prove to be important. No one factor in and of itself led to Nixon's resignation from the Presidency of the United States. Factors in the resignation seemed to include a decrease in congressional support and popularity among the public, potential financial ruin (if impeached he would lose retirement and support income), the embarrassment of a Senate trial, loss of contact with presidential aides who were close to Nixon and appeared to provide him with emotional support, and fear of prosecution for Watergate-related crimes. As another example of the complexity of social causation, consider the factors that may influence a person to go to college. He or she may go to obtain a high-paying or prestigious job. But one of these factors alone obviously is not sufficient to explain college attendance. Perhaps opportunity and personal desire must be considered as additional factors in a more complete assessment.

Explanations of social events based on multiple causes requires the development of complex theories of human behavior. These theories may prove to be *additive,* that is, the effects of the causal factors are independent and accumulate together to produce the overall effect on the dependent variable. To illustrate the additive model in a rough way, let us suppose loss of status somehow accounts for "half" of a person's suicide and personal stress accounts for the other half. In an additive model (assuming loss of status and personal stress are independent of one another) these separate effects may combine to account for the suicide. This illustrates only one possible way separate effects may produce an event in an additive way; additive theories can take a variety of forms.

Rather than such "simple" additive models, theories of social behavior may be *interactive* in nature. Such nonadditive models are basically more complex and more difficult to test than additive models. In suicide, an example of an interactive model is the case where the degree of loss of status and the degree of personal stress combine in a surprising way to produce an effect. Suppose a small loss in status, combined with severe personal stress, increases the probability of suicide to a greater level than a large loss of status and severe personal stress. This is not consistent with an additive model. Somehow the two states (small loss of status and severe stress) combine to produce an effect of greater magnitude than expected.

A *threshold effect* is another example of nonadditivity if two variables interact to produce an event. A threshold effect exists if no change occurs in a dependent variable until a specified level is reached in an independent variable. This is the case if a person's change in living style from "middle" to "upper" class occurs only when an income of $50,000 or more is reached (an increase from say $30,000 to $45,000 does not produce a change); or perhaps stress is unrelated to suicide until it reaches an extremely severe level.

Theories of social behavior may be even more complex than this; some may involve a *feedback principle.* In a feedback theory the independent and dependent variables work back and forth on one another. The causal direction may initially be from the independent variables to the dependent variable; but, once a change occurs in the dependent variable, it causes changes in the independent variables. Income may initially determine one's educational level; but once a certain educational level is obtained, it may determine one's income. Initially an increasing crime rate in a city may partially determine an increase in the size of its police force. A larger police force, in turn, may increase the crime rate because a larger number of policemen is available to arrest more people.

Multiple causation, additivity, interaction, and feedback illustrate some of the difficulties of establishing causes of social events.

POTENTIAL BIASES AND LIMITATIONS IN STUDYING HUMAN BEHAVIOR   The fact that in the social sciences human beings study human beings creates possible biases in establishing relations between variables and in establishing causes of events. How events are observed, recorded, and interpreted is related to a person's beliefs, opinions, attitudes, and training (among other

factors). We see things through "tinted glasses" based on sociali-
zation in our environments. We selectively perceive what happens around us, and such selectivity is learned. What we are
taught to see may not be the causal factors. If so, scientists may
have to first "unlearn," or at least learn to see things in new ways.

Besides being limited by selective perception, as social
scientists we also can become emotionally involved in our subject
matter (see the section on participant observation in Chapter 5).
In trying to describe a social situation (crowd behavior at a
sporting event, a political rally, a doctor-patient relationship, a
lovers' quarrel), we may be so close to it that we cannot see its
important characteristics. We may get involved in the very
situation we are observing and thereby actually change the
situation by our presence; or in studying a work group we may
influence its productivity simply by our presence; or we may
find out how a small community handles its problems only when
a social scientist is studying it. It is often necessary to have
explicit rules on how to observe a social situation and on what
factors to consider to be able to reduce such "side effects."

In some of the classic ESP (extrasensory perception)
studies, a different but related kind of bias occurred. Apparently
those observers who believed in ESP found positive results
(supporting the existence of ESP), while those who did not
believe in ESP found negative results. The negative results were
even beyond chance to the point where study results showed a
reverse effect to the existence of ESP. To illustrate, let us
suppose a person who is assumed to have ESP is placed in a
situation where he or she guesses whether a card contains an
odd or an even number. If the person truly has ESP, he or she
should be able to tell better than 50 percent of the time (that is,
better than chance) whether the card contains an odd or an even
number. It has been found that the results of some ESP studies
depend on the beliefs of the researchers. If the researchers
believe in ESP, they find correct answers over 50 percent of the
time; if researchers do not believe in ESP, they find less than 50
percent of the answers are correct. Now if ESP does not exist, a
person should do no worse than chance (right 50 percent of the

time and wrong 50 percent of the time). Here is an obvious case of bias in human beings studying other human beings.

Although only speculative, the ESP case may apply to the recent "findings" on the sensitivity of plants. Supposedly there are observations that certain plants "know" what happens around them. If a person cuts and kills a neighboring plant in a room, the other plants will respond to that person in a different way in subsequent visits. This is not to deny that plants have the capability of being turned off by human "killers," but apparently only persons who believe in "thinking" plants have carried out the research.

Such potential observational bias may extend to testing hypotheses. Some social scientists may become so emotionally involved in the rationales, ideas, and hypotheses they develop that they want them to be true. When they are studying them and trying to determine their validity or invalidity, subtle biases may operate to produce supporting results. Whenever an error is made, it is likely to be in the direction of confirmation rather than negation.

There are ways of reducing the effects of such biasing factors. When conducting a study, a social scientist can let "naive" assistants do the actual observing and analysis; these assistants are not told the true nature of the study or the hypotheses. This assumes that what they do not know will not hurt them or the study. Explicitly stated measuring procedures, measuring instruments (scales, rulers, etc.), and clearly stated research guidelines all should operate to reduce such biases.

Another problem in determining the causes of human behavior is the limitations imposed on the researcher in using people as units of analysis. People cannot be planted in different types of soil, they cannot be given lethal doses of drugs, and they cannot be morally violated—this list can be extended to a much greater length. Simply stated, certain experiments are taboo. We cannot study the effects of cigarette smoking by selecting a group of five-year-olds and inducing the habit.

The limitations in studying people extend to the interview situation. Some people do not want to be studied, and except in such places as concentration camps there is no legal way of making them participate. Those who refuse to be interviewed or who will not fill out questionnaires tend to be different from those who do. If we base our generalizations solely on those who are willing to be studied, we are likely to overgeneralize ("going beyond the data"). The results of such studies simply do not characterize all people.

For the above reasons, we must be constantly on guard for biases and limitations in studying people. A promising research strategy is to use a variety of techniques in studying any particular social phenomenon. Perhaps all the techniques have some biases, but the different techniques may have different biases. If different techniques with different biases produce similar results, some confidence can be placed in generalizations about human behavior.

summary

To achieve the major goal of science, which is to establish causal laws, facts and relations between variables must be established. The criteria to establish facts and relations are the procedures of the scientific method. This method is based on careful and reliable observation.

There are four widely accepted scientific criteria for establishing causality: association, time priority, nonspurious relation, and rationale. The magnitude and consistency of an association are two characteristics that generally strengthen the conclusion that one variable is at least the partial cause of another. Time priority refers to the case where the independent variable either occurs first or changes prior to the dependent variable. Establishing a time priority among variables depends on the logic of the situation, on observation, on theory, and on data analysis. A nonspurious relation refers to the situation where the effects of a third variable are eliminated and the relation between the independent and dependent variables is maintained. Finally, the rationale refers to theory, explanation, or interpretation of a relation that stipulates that not only does the independent variable change first, but it also causes changes in the dependent variable.

references

Brownlee, K. A. 1965. "A Review of 'Smoking and Health.'" *Journal of the American Statistical Association,* **60:**722–740.

Gibbs, Jack P. 1972. *Sociological Theory Construction.* Hinsdale, Ill.: Dryden Press.

Hirschi, Travis, and Hanna C. Selvin. 1967. *Delinquency Research.* Glencoe, Ill.: The Free Press of Glencoe, Inc.

Hyman, Herbert H. 1955. *Survey Design and Analysis.* Glencoe, Ill.: The Free Press of Glencoe, Inc.

Kaplan, Abraham. 1964. *The Conduct of Inquiry.* San Francisco: Chandler Publishing Company.

Kuhn, Thomas S. 1970. *The Structure of Scientific Revolutions.* 2nd ed., International Encyclopedia of Unified Science, vol. 2, number 2, Chicago, Ill.: University of Chicago Press.

Pelz, Donald C., and Frank M. Andrews. 1964. "Detecting Causal Priorities in Panel Study Data." *American Sociological Review,* **29:**836–848.

Simon, Julian. 1969. *Basic Research Methods in Social Science: The Art of Empirical Investigation.* New York: Random House, Chapter 26.

Stephens, William N. 1968. *Hypotheses and Evidence.* New York: Thomas Y. Crowell Company.

Selection and Conceptual Formulation of the Problem

This chapter outlines some of the basic sources used in formulating research problems. The research problem is the first in a series of steps defining the scientific method. Chapters 2 through 6 set up the method and lead the student step-by-step through some actual research studies. The steps are as follows: first, the research problem (Chapter 2); second, the conceptual framework (Chapter 2); third, the population and sample (Chapter 3); fourth, the research design (Chapter 4); fifth, the methods of observation (Chapter 5); and sixth, data analysis (Chapter 6).

Social-research problems range from descriptive accounts to testing the validity of hypotheses. The methods of social research include small, loosely designed, exploratory investigations, highly structured national surveys, observation of "natural" events, and the analysis of contrived experimental settings. The selection from the wide range of social-research techniques is closely tied to the kind of research problem in question.

the research problem

There are a variety of sources for research ideas. These sources include individual experiences, hunches, written material (books, monographs, and journals), personal conversation, research findings, values, or theory. In the case of theory, the research problem is derived from a set of related statements. Actually, ideas leading to constructive research come from almost any source. Probably, the most theoretically relevant ideas come from research findings and discussions with others in the discipline.

One source for a research problem is the researcher's values. For example, if an individual believes that the democratic system is best, he may test the hypothesis that democratically structured small groups will have the most success in completing tasks or will have the highest rates of loyalty. Another individual, believing in the virtues of strong totalitarian leadership, may hypothesize that groups with appointed leaders who are given nearly complete power will have the most success in completing tasks or will have the highest rates of loyalty.

There is nothing wrong, from the standpoint of the scientific method, with testing ideas resulting from personal values, as long as biases are controlled in carrying out the research. Presumably, the two hypothetical researchers described above could design and carry out similar studies to test their hypotheses. A properly designed study will yield results that are not influenced by the researcher's values, even though his values may have influenced the selection of the problem.

Consistent findings or statistical associations often lead to further research of theoretical ideas. For example, Emile Durkheim (1951) noted that certain countries, such as Denmark (largely Protestant), persist in having high rates of suicide, while others, such as Italy (largely Catholic), have low suicide rates. From such observations, Durkheim surmised that suicide varied by religion, with Protestants having higher rates than Catholics. These observations were conceptualized into theoretical statements about the effects of social integration or group solidarity on suicide incidence. One of his major propositions is that the suicide rate varies inversely with the degree of social integration.

Besides consistency, surprise or inconsistent findings or associations may lead to fruitful ideas in research. Robert K. Merton (1957), in a study of the small suburban community of Craftown, found that parents, although in an area with relatively few baby sitters, felt that there were more sitters than there were in their previous urban residences, where there were actually many more potential sitters. These suburbanites felt more at ease and trusted teenagers more than they did when they lived in the city. Thus, Merton suggests, the perceived number of available baby sitters apparently does not depend entirely on the actual number, but on trust. Craftown is a comparatively cohesive community, characterized by intimate contact with others. Consequently, the perception of the number of available sitters depended upon the trust placed in possessing the intimate knowledge of others in a cohesive community. From this, Merton concluded that perception depends upon the structure of human relations.

Another example of unexpected findings leading to fruitful discoveries comes from a study by Samuel A. Stouffer et al. (1949), who observed that during World War II soldiers in military units with high rates of promotion actually felt they had less chance for promotion than did soldiers in units with lower rates. Furthermore, comparing units at home with those overseas, the researchers found that differences in attitudes on such topics as satisfaction with army life and the efficiency with which the army is run were *not* large. They expected quite different findings, because most men overseas had an overriding concern just to get back home. To explain these results the researchers hypothesized that soldiers were comparing themselves to specific significant others, and they came up with the idea of *relative deprivation,* which has proved to be an important concept in later studies. For example, soldiers overseas, perhaps, compared themselves with those overseas in combat and so felt themselves not to be deprived; and, perhaps, soldiers at home compared themselves with those overseas and consequently were not so unhappy. The concept of relative deprivation also clarified the findings about promotion. Evidently, soldiers in military units with high promotion rates felt deprived relative to the large number of men in their units who were promoted. Those in low promotion units apparently did not feel as deprived.

The ideas for a study by Charles E. Bowerman and Glen H. Elder (1964) apparently were an outgrowth of several empirical studies of family structure. The researchers noted that the results of these studies were inconsistent and that these inconsistencies could be due to the differential treatment of family structure. For example, some studies treated the conjugal balance of power (between husband and wife), while others stressed parental power in child-rearing relations. Bowerman and Elder made these different aspects of family structure conceptually distinct. Their research problem, in part, was to find the effects of the distinct family structural patterns on the scholastic motivation and college plans of adolescents. In a more recent study by Elder (1965) on a similar but more restricted topic, the research problem was to assess the effects of parental dominance on the development of achievement potential. Both of these studies will be cited throughout this book as illustrations of the different steps in the scientific method.

Once an investigator comes up with a researchable idea, whatever its source, he should familiarize himself with past and current thought and research in the area. It is usually desirable to discuss the idea with colleagues and to review the literature concerned with anything related to the topic. Knowing what has been done can benefit the researcher by (1) warning him of unfruitful leads that have been taken in past research, (2) clarifying the dimensions of the topic in question, and (3) suggesting the variety of ways the major concepts can be observed. When these tasks are accomplished, the researcher is likely to be in a position to make meaningful tests of his hypotheses.

conceptual framework

An adequate conceptual framework of social phenomena is necessary to present the research problem in terms of a clear and testable statement. Vague ideas will lead to inadequate and uninterpretable research findings. Consequently, important variables should be defined clearly and at least some should be operationally defined (as described below) to permit testable propositions. Besides well-defined variables, the conceptual framework of a study includes relational statements linking two or more variables (or hypotheses) and theoretical rationales specifying how and why the variables and relational statements are interrelated.

      To illustrate the nature of a theoretical rationale, consider the relations between education, occupational prestige, income, and radicalism (George Caspar Homans, 1961). Let us assume that persons who have invested in several years of education (for example, physicians and dentists) will expect high occupational prestige and income later on. Suppose, however, that the investment (in terms of years of education) is perceived as too high a price for the resulting rewards of occupational prestige or income. Ministers, college professors, and social workers illustrate these high-educational-investment–low-prestige-and-income occupations. Based on the assumption that those who perceive that they are not receiving their just rewards in society will most want to change the structure of society, we can hypothesize the following: (1) high-investment–low-reward occupations have a greater percentage of persons with radical beliefs than low-investment–high-reward or equal investment-reward occupations; and (2) high-investment–low-reward occupations have a greater percentage of persons who participate in demonstrations, sign petitions, and vote for changes in the legal system than low-investment–high-reward or equal investment-reward occupations.

The theoretical rationale based on the ideas of investments and rewards specifies and justifies the nature of the relations between the variables of education, occupational prestige, income, and radicalism. Although theoretically justified, the hypotheses need to be empirically tested and verified before they can be accepted as valid.

It should be noted that there are many exploratory and descriptive studies in sociology that are not based on logically developed theoretical rationales. These studies often are preliminary to the development of verified theory.

CONCEPTS   Human thought is characterized by the use of language, which includes symbols and rules for their combination. That is, communication is formulated symbolically. One symbol of special importance is the *concept.* To obtain the knowledge of any field of study requires, at the outset, an intimate and extensive acquaintance with its concepts. Crucial to learning the concepts is acquiring their definitions, meanings, applications, and interrelations. A concept is a term or symbol that represents the similarities in otherwise diverse phenomena. For example, although men vary among themselves in many of their individual traits, all are classified in the category of "mammal" on the basis of similarities in certain biological characteristics.

Besides the concept, another term of equal importance is the *variable.* A variable is a measurable dimension of a concept (for example, the height of males) or a measurable concept (biological differences between males and females) that takes on two or more values, either from one unit (individual or group) to the next or for any unit at different periods of time. For example, men vary in terms of height and weight; and from one time period to another an individual may grow or put on weight.

Sociology is rich in the number of concepts with which it works—for example, status, role, norm, value, interaction, and relative deprivation. Any one of these concepts may be studied as a variable if measured in some way. For example, *status* is a term that we encounter in both sociological and popular writings. Both sociologists and the lay public use a classification of occupational prestige as a rough index of status. A high status may be indicated by a high-prestige occupation such as that of a doctor; and the reverse would be a low status, indicated by a low-prestige occupation such as that of a prostitute.

The development of concepts, which are products of reasoning, requires two processes: *generalizing* and *abstracting*. Generalizing is the process of deriving a principle from a variety of experiences, such as a child noting that a tree can come in many shapes and sizes. Any variable or concept necessarily represents an abstraction; that is, they include only selected features of the phenomenon in question. These features are held in common by certain units or individuals, which places them in a category. To give an example of a sociological concept, *role performance* refers solely to those behavior patterns of individuals that are dictated by the social roles they occupy. Students take exams, show up for lectures, take notes, participate in class at times, and turn in homework assignments. Only these activities are included in the role performance of students. Many other activities that may happen to involve some students are not included—for example, interaction with siblings and parents, dating, leisure time activities, and working during the summer. In short, the role performance of students is an abstraction from the total activities of students of only those activities dictated by that particular role.

DEFINITIONS   Communication, in the sense of one person understanding another, is dependent upon the sharing of the same meaning of the symbols or concepts used. The

meanings of our symbols come from their definitions. A definition is a statement of intention to use a symbol in a specified way;
that is, a definition tells what a term means. For example, one
definition of "suicide" is to kill yourself or to fail to save yourself
when you can.

It should be noted that definitions are *not* scientific laws.
The statement that "self-destruction varies directly with suicide"
does nothing more than substitute the words "self-destruction"
for "suicide." The statement is true by definition (not by
observation or testing) and does not constitute a scientific law or
even evidence leading to a scientific law.

Definitions also do not comprise any type of fundamen-
tal truths or truth statements, because definitions are arbitrary.
Being arbitrary, definitions are neither right nor wrong, true
nor false. For example, to say that "the human mind is the
central nervous system and that alone" is not wrong. It is merely
a statement of intention to use the term in a specified way.
Consider, further, the concept of "love." To say that love is
sexual interaction and nothing more is not a false or wrong (or
true or right) statement. Words mean what you define them to
mean. That is, meanings assigned to words or concepts are in a
sense arbitrary. When we talk about definitions, we are usually
referring to the common or conventional meanings of words.
That is, definitions, such as those found in dictionaries, are the
conventional meanings of words. For this reason, such definitions are not true or false, but rather, they are conventional or
unconventional. To say that a definition is false is only to say that
it is unconventional.

Technically, there are two basic types of definitions,
nominal and *operational.* Nominal definitions are used in cases
where a given word is to be synonymous with certain other
expressions, the meanings of which are already established. The
previous definitions of the human mind and love are nominal
definitions. A further example would be to define
"interpersonal attraction," a much-used term in social psychology, as "to draw to" or "cause to approach." In this last example,
we are saying that "attraction" is synonymous with "to draw to"

or "cause to approach." In this type of definition, the defining terms can substitute for the word defined. The advantage of such definitions is that they provide a shorthand method of communication. For example, rather than say, "A given word is to be synonymous with certain other expressions whose meaning is already established," we say, "A nominal definition."

The second type of definition is operational. An operational definition is the specification of the observable procedures used to identify the referent of the term defined. A variable is operationally defined if the steps in its observation or measurement are clearly stated. If a clear operational definition is given, reliable results can be obtained. Without reliable results, we can never be sure of our facts; and if the facts are in doubt, we cannot know if a hypothesis is proved or disproved. *Reliability* is established when two or more competent observers (within specified limits) come up with the same results when measuring the same phenomenon. For example, measuring the height of a specified individual by a ruler yields highly similar results among different observers. In this instance, height is operationally defined as the number of inches from the head to the foot, as measured by a ruler.

Operational definitions are oriented toward the empirical world—that is, phenomena that are observable. Therefore, to operationalize the idea of a "good student" one could specify all undergraduates with a grade-point average of 3.0 or above, or to use a different set of goals, all students who are absent less than five times per semester or quarter. Furthermore, with relatively few instructions, competent observers can count the number of absences or compute the GPA in order to classify a student as "good" or "not good." The results then have a high probability of being reliable.

In research, there are several problems involved in formulating operational definitions. One problem is to define the phenomena in question. To illustrate, consider the problem of evaluating the feelings that members of a particularly close-knit group, such as a jazz combo or a small sorority, have toward each other. Sociologists describe this feeling by using the concept of *group solidarity,* which may be nominally defined as the strength of positive interpersonal relations between individuals. The problem is to spell out clearly the procedure to measure this strength. How can positive sentiment (feeling) between group members be measured? How can we tell if one group has more solidarity than another? One way is to ask the members who they like and dislike in their group. The group that, as a whole, indicates the greater number of likes, or the largest ratio of likes to dislikes, is considered to have higher group solidarity. Another approach is to consider attendance or participation at group meetings as measures of solidarity. Perhaps groups in which most members attend or participate in meetings exhibit greater solidarity than groups where few attend or participate.

If group solidarity is measured in terms of positive sentiments displayed by members at group meetings, the operational problem is to tell observers what is meant by a "positive sentiment." We could count up the number of times members smile or ask about the health and welfare of other members, but would we be willing to classify all such responses as positive sentiments? Should polite smiles be counted, and can we distinguish between "polite" and "genuine" smiles? These problems are intensified in cross-cultural research where, for example, in some societies smiles may not be an expression of positive sentiment.

A second major problem involved in operationalizing concepts is to identify the competent observers. For example, most adults can measure your weight or height, but how much training is necessary before a person is competent to administer an intelligence test? If normal people are needed to administer questionnaires or to interview respondents, how do you distinguish the normal from the abnormal? Psychiatrists and clinical psychologists often disagree among themselves on whether or not an individual is neurotic or psychotic, let alone on identification of the mental illness involved.

One dominant way sociologists operationally define variables is by items in questionnaires and interviews. One operational measure of social class is simply to ask respondents to place themselves in a class by checking one of the categories of upper, middle, or lower class. Bowerman and Elder (1964) determined the conjugal power structure of families by asking respondents (white adolescents) the question: "When important family problems come up, which parent usually has the most *influence* in making the decision?" If a respondent indicated that the mother had the most influence the family was classified as wife-dominant; if the father was designated, it was classified as husband-dominant; and if both parents were mentioned, the family was classified as equalitarian. It must be pointed out, however, that power relationships within the family are often misperceived and other measures of power may yield different answers.

A sound research strategy for some studies is to use two or more different operational definitions for one variable. Suppose we wanted to clearly specify the leaders of a small community. One way of operationalizing leadership, that is, of discovering who are the decision makers or power wielders in a community, is to find out who holds the important positions in the major organizations. Those individuals may be designated as high on leadership who are members of executive boards, are in top management positions in business enterprises, or hold high ranking offices in the government or military. An operational definition of leadership, consequently, is based on the positions a person occupies in important organizations in the community. To carry out a leadership study based on organizational position it is necessary to obtain (1) a list of the major organizations, (2) a list of the top positions in each, and (3) a list of personnel occupying these positions.

A different operational definition of leadership is contingent upon the reputation of community members. In interviews with a few key informants from the community, we could ask, "Who runs this community?" or "If a hospital (or school) were to be built, who would decide its cost and location?" The names given in response to such questions constitute the community leaders (at least by reputation).

A third way to operationally define leadership is to measure the degree of social participation of community members. People who join many community organizations, who hold offices and do committee work in such organizations, who attend meetings, who vote in elections, and who contribute to community drives will rank high on this measure of leadership. Those who stay out of community affairs will rank low. The actual operational definition of leadership as social participation may be based on the researcher's direct observations or on asking respondents such questions as: "Which organizations in the community do you belong to?"; "Do you hold offices (attend meetings, serve on committees) in these organizations?"; "Did you vote in the last election?"; and "Did you contribute to the last community drive?"

To grasp the idea of operational definitions, you should try to draft a few. Can you specify clearly how you might measure a "democratic" society, a "mature" person, an "industrialized" area, a "happy" family, or a "prejudiced" person?

INDICATORS Many variables in the social sciences are quite abstract and general. To permit a scientific study of an abstract and general variable, a clearly defined indicator or several indicators are selected that link it to observation. Leadership, discussed above, is an example of this type of variable. Leadership may have several dimensions: position, reputation, decision-making ability, social participation. To operationalize all dimensions usually is beyond the resources of a single study. The researcher, consequently, may select one (or more) indicators of leadership. He or she may consider only position or only social participation. The leadership variable still remains general and abstract; the indicators link it to the observational world and allow us to study it scientifically.

The choice of indicators depends on the availability of information, the likelihood of obtaining certain kinds of information, and the theory guiding the researcher. If the suicide rate for a particular country is not tabulated, we simply cannot use such information as an indicator of social disorganization or degree of personal stress. If people refuse to answer questions about their sex life, we cannot use frequency of coitus as an indicator of marital harmony. If our theory assumes that reality resides in the minds of respondents, answers to the question "Are you in the upper, middle, or lower class?" are indicators of social-class position.

Indicators are useful if concepts are vague or if direct measures are not available. Age is defined directly as number of years since birth. Suppose we wanted to establish the relative youth or old age of a population and did not have access to birth dates. We can use the percentage of the population in secondary schools as an indicator of the age of the population (if such information is available). A small percentage indicates an older population, and a high percentage a younger population. Another indicator of age is the number of facial wrinkles. In general, older people have more wrinkles than younger people. Obviously these indicators are imprecise. Some people develop wrinkles at earlier ages than others, and there may be a variety of reasons why a society has a low percentage of its population in secondary schools, for example, poverty and negative feelings about formal education.

RELATION OF SCIENTIFIC TERMS TO THE EMPIRICAL WORLD   As stated previously, scientific concepts of one class are directly linked to observable phenomena by the use of operational definitions; scientific concepts of another class are stated in terms of nominal definitions and are not linked to observables. Often, scientific concepts are both nominally and operationally defined. A major problem in the social sciences concerns the relation between the nominal definitions and the operational definitions. For example, suppose "aggression" is nominally defined as "hurting others," and operationally defined as "the number of times one person hits or throws things at another." The operational definition leaves out the subtle psychological forms of hurting (verbal aggression, insults, ribbing, teasing, etc.) that are implied in the nominal definition. Although there are serious problems in obtaining meaningful operational definitions that adequately reflect (are isomorphic with) the nominal definitions, linking a concept to the empirical world is crucial to the development of science. In evaluating research, it is important to check the researcher's measures of a concept. Two scientists investigating the consequences of power may reach contradictory conclusions because they operationalized the concept in different ways.

VALIDITY   To secure validity we need to establish the true dimension of a variable or to determine a true relation between variables. A *valid measure* truly reflects the theoretically defined dimension of a variable, and a *valid relationship* truly depicts the association between two or more variables. The extent to which both types of validity (measurement and relationship) are established is only approximated in the social sciences.

Ideally the validity of a measuring instrument is determined by comparing it to a well-defined and theoretically supported standard measure. If you want to know if your 12-inch ruler is accurate (that is, a valid measure of 1 foot), compare its length to an agreed upon standard 12-inch ruler. The critical problem in the social sciences is that well-established measures do not exist for major variables. Measurements of variables, consequently, cannot be compared to such a valid (true) measure.

In the absence of this preferred way, two indirect techniques may be used to approximate the validity of a measure: (1) prediction of an outside criterion and (2) theoretically meaningful results.

Would the proportion of students who do not vote in campus elections be a valid measure of student apathy? Suppose we find in comparing several universities that as the proportion of nonvoters increases, grade-point average decreases and absenteeism from class increases. On the basis of prediction of outside criteria (GPA and absenteeism) the measure is valid. However, in terms of theoretically meaningful results or face validity the measure may or may not be valid. If you feel in accordance with some theory that the purpose of a university is student self-fulfillment, voting in campus elections may not be an apathetic response. Theoretically, whether or not you vote may have nothing to do with apathy. According to one rationale, student apathy exists only if students drop out in large numbers.

The establishment of a valid relationship between variables involves three dimensions: (1) valid measures of each variable, (2) unbiased research designs, and (3) a representative sample of the population under consideration. There are several sociological studies that show a direct relationship between socioeconomic status (SES) and community participation. SES may be measured by income, by occupational prestige, or by education (or some combination of these three), and community participation may be measured by responses to the question "Which organizations in this community do you belong to and/or hold office in?" To establish whether these measures of SES and community participation are valid, we could attempt to predict an outside criterion variable with each (as with student apathy) or determine if they make sense according to some theory. An unbiased research design enables us to conclude that the direct relationship is not due to biases or limitations of the study (on this issue see Chapter 4, "Research Design"). If we wish to infer the direct relationship to a specific population (all the people in a particular city or country), it is necessary to have a representative sample (or the whole population). Random sampling (as discussed in Chapter 3) is a reasonable technique for establishing representativeness.

UTILITY OF SCIENTIFIC CONCEPTS Useful concepts should be formed into predictive and causal statements. That is, concepts should be defined in ways that lead to the testing of hypotheses and the building of sound theories. Definitions leading to supported hypotheses and comprehensive theories are superior to those that do not. For example, Bowerman and Elder (1964) observed that past studies of family structure often confused the effects of the conjugal balance of power (husband-wife) with parental power (father-mother) in the child-rearing relationship. By conceptually and operationally distinguishing between these two sources of power, they were able to assess the independent predictive ability of each in a variety of variables, including the child's motivation to attend college.

A useful scientific concept without predictive power is natural selection (survival of the fittest). With a knowledge of natural selection alone, we are unable to predict which of several species will survive in an environment. Natural selection has been used after the fact; we observe which species have survived and define these as the best adapted to their environments. Those that died out, by definition, were not the fittest. Although this concept's predictive ability is nil, its classificatory and heuristic abilities have been extensive. Partly on the basis of natural selection (and partly on genetic inheritance and mutation), species of birds, animals, insects, fish, and plants have been grouped into meaningful categories. Historical connections between different species have been well established. We can make such statements as "humans are more closely related to the baboon than to the horse," and "the ancestors of all animal life go back to life in the sea."

Many concepts in everyday language are used to "explain" and "predict"; for example, "Wars are caused by an aggressive instinct," or "He has tantrums because he is an only child and is spoiled because his parents are too permissive." These may be referred to as common-sense explanations, although they are not necessarily predictive or explanatory from a scientific point of view.

In science, cause is based on rigorous criteria. As described in Chapter 1, the four criteria for causation are as follows: non-zero association, time priority, nonspurious relation, and theoretical rationale.

PRECISION OF SCIENTIFIC CONCEPTS   In the initial stages of the development of a scientific discipline, descriptions and generalizations are stated in the vocabulary of everyday language. The growth of science brings with it the development of specialized concepts and a technical terminology. In this sense, the development of a science is dependent upon the increased precision of its concepts to describe and explain. For example, *socioeconomic status* (based on measurable dimensions of prestige, income, and education) is a more precise concept than its forerunner of *social class,* which is usually conceptualized in a rather general and vague manner.

Usually, scientific concepts are made more precise (that is, the number of meanings of a concept is reduced) by giving an everyday language concept a concise and limited nominal definition and then operationalizing the concept to link dimensions directly to the empirical world. An empirical study is conducted to determine the utility of the concept. If a hypothesis (containing the concept as an independent or dependent variable) is disconfirmed, a new operational definition may be tested, or the concept may be dropped as not useful in a predictive sense. If the hypothesis is confirmed, the utility of the concept is established, or if partially confirmed, attempts to redefine the concept more adequately may be undertaken.

For example, consider the issue over the degree to which Americans are religious, or the degree to which religion has "declined" in America recently. There might be general agreement that Americans, compared with members of other nations, are not very religious. This, however, is not adequate evidence for science, because religiosity has several meanings. What does it mean to have persons agree that Americans are not very religious? Religiosity may be nominally defined as believing in and following the rules of one's religion; but to determine the degree of religiosity in the American population, the concept must be operationally defined. Following the nominal definition, we might end up with a scale of religiosity like that recently developed by Joseph E. Faulkner and Gordon F. De Jong

(1962). Based on twenty-four questionnaire items, their scale is built on five dimensions: ideological, intellectual, ritualistic, experiential, and consequential. Examples of their questions are: "Do you believe the world will come to an end according to the will of God?" "How do you personally view the story of creation as recorded in Genesis?" "How much time during a week would you say you spend reading the Bible and other religious literature?"

THEORETICAL RATIONALES AND RELATIONAL STATEMENTS

Scientific concepts are necessary for the development of rationales and relational statements. The basic goal of science is to validate theory and establish scientific laws. The testable assertions of theory usually are labeled *hypotheses.*[1] In sociology, widely validated hypotheses have yet to be found. Some limited hypotheses, not nearly as specific as the laws of the physical sciences, have been partially proved under certain conditions. These comprise the knowledge of sociology, which is certainly not as advanced a discipline as physics, astronomy, or biology.

To illustrate, let us cite three examples of sociological hypotheses.

1. The suicide rate varies inversely with status integration (the degree to which simultaneously occupied statuses do not have conflicting expectations).
2. Urbanization is positively associated with the number of voluntary organizations in an area.
3. High educational attainment is most prevalent

---

[1] Scientific statements are tentative rather than absolute. Relations between variables that have been firmly established may be negated by further evidence. Changes or different circumstances may invalidate a scientific law or force limitations on its generality. That X is related to Y in all experiments performed is no assurance that the relation will hold in future experiments. It is the nature of scientific statements that they are subject to continuous testing. Consequently, the confirmation of any theory, law, or hypothesis is a matter of degree rather than absolute certainty.

among persons who report democratic relations with their parents and equalitarian relations between mother and father.

Note that these partially supported hypotheses are not characterized by the precise mathematical formulas of the laws of the physical sciences. This is a rough indicator of our state of knowledge in sociology. The field is well beyond total ignorance of social phenomena, but far short of the spectacular development of the physical sciences.

Consequently, the logical-deductive structure of theory seldom applies to sociology. In its place, sociologists often use rather brief theoretical rationales. These rationales usually constitute anywhere from a paragraph to several pages of discussion stating reasons why two or more variables are related in a certain way (hypotheses).

For example, consider the fact that urban areas have more voluntary organizations, such as civic organizations and social clubs, than do rural areas. The rationale for this assertion may involve the following: In cities there are fewer interpersonal relationships that are important to the urbanite; on the average, family size is smaller; and less importance is attached to the extended family. Consequently city dwellers compensate for fewer personal contacts in these areas by joining and participating in community organizations, where they can extend their contacts. The rationale does not represent a rigorous deductive structure, but it does provide some justification for expecting those in urban areas to join more voluntary organizations than do those in rural areas.

Sociological theory is decidedly at the age of modest theoretical rationales and testable working hypotheses. A hypothesis is an empirically testable statement of the relation between two or more variables. To be empirical (i.e., subject to observation) the variables must be operationally defined.

The student should be warned that there are very few examples of logical-theory structure in the sociological literature. Perhaps this rigid structure is premature in a discipline without a substantial empirical base and only comes later, as it did in physics and astronomy, after many sound and replicated observations have been made.

summary

Concepts and variables are crucial to the development of science. A concept is a term or symbol that describes the similarities in otherwise diverse phenomena. A variable is a measurable concept or a measurable dimension of a concept that takes on two or more values. An example of a concept is "status," which can be changed to a variable by measuring occupational prestige.

It is important to distinguish between nominal and operational definitions. Nominal definitions state that a given word is to be synonymous with certain other expressions, the meanings of which are already established. An operational definition is the specification of the observable procedures used to identify the referent of the term defined. To illustrate the difference between the two types of definitions, a nominal definition of status is the prestige level of specified occupational groups. Status may be operationally defined by self-placement into high, medium, and low occupational prestige categories.

Operational definitions link concepts to the empirical world, which is necessary for testing hypotheses. The utility of a scientific concept is assessed in terms of its role in testing hypotheses and in constructing theories. Concepts must be precise to be used in testing hypotheses and in constructing theories. In this sense, the development of science is dependent upon increased precision of the concepts used to describe and explain.

The use of concepts in logical deductive theories is rare in sociology. In its place, sociologists use theoretical rationales that explain why they expect variables to be related in a certain way. In these rationales, the terms are defined operationally and the relations between concepts are specified.

references

Bowerman, Charles E., and Glen H. Elder. 1964. "Variations in Adolescent Perception in Family Power Structure." *American Sociological Review,* **29:**551–567.

Durkheim, Emile. 1951. *Suicide.* Glencoe, Ill.: The Free Press of Glencoe, Inc.

Elder, Glen H. 1965. "Family Structure and Educational Attainment: A Cross-National Analysis." *American Sociological Review,* **30:**81–96.

Faulkner, Joseph E., and Gordon F. De Jong. 1962. "Religiosity in 5-D: An Empirical Analysis." *Social Forces,* **45:**246–254 (December).

Gibbs, Jack P. 1972. *Sociological Theory Construction.* Hinsdale, Ill.: Dryden Press.

Homans, George Caspar. 1961. *Social Behavior: Its Elementary Forms.* New York: Harcourt, Brace & World, Inc. (This discussion is based on the author's concept of distributive justice; see chapter 12.)

Kaplan, Abraham. 1964. *The Conduct of Inquiry.* San Francisco: Chandler Publishing Company.

Lundberg, George A., Clarence C. Schrag, Otto N. Larsen, and William R. Catton, Jr. 1968. *Sociology.* 4th ed. New York: Harper & Row, Publishers. Chapter 2.

Merton, Robert K. 1957. *Social Theory and Social Structure.* Rev. ed. Glencoe, Ill.: The Free Press of Glencoe, Inc. Chapters 2, 3, 8, and 9.

Stouffer, Samuel A., et al. 1949. *The American Soldier.* Vol. 1. Princeton, N.J.: Princeton University Press.

Chapter 3

Population
and Sampling

The *population* (or universe) refers to the largest body of individuals (or other units) being researched: for example, industrialized societies, urban riots, delinquents, college students, or infants. In the final analysis, the researcher wants to say something about the population. A crucial step in social research is to define the population clearly; a clearly defined population makes the selection of representative samples more probable. Such samples are used to infer characteristics of the part (sample) to the whole (population). In statistical terms, the conclusions of a study are restricted to the specified population. For example, if in 1975 you studied delinquents in Ohio, your statistically based conclusions are restricted exclusively to Ohio delinquents (at that particular point in time). The results may apply to delinquents from other states, but to an unknown degree. Further research is required before inferences may be made to other areas or to a larger or different number of individuals or units.

sampling

A scientist seldom observes a total population, but usually gathers data on a part or *sample.* He then tries to specify something about the population from knowledge of the sample (that is, he infers from one to the other). Some populations can never be studied directly because of lack of accessibility, limited time, or prohibitive cost. For example, no one is presently capable of organizing a study of all inhabitants in the world. Furthermore, certain types of problems require destructive procedures that destroy the unit tested. We would not want to use the total population of electric light bulbs to test their life span, and we would want no more than a small quantity of blood out of the human body to test for the presence of a rare disease (or for that matter, no more than a sample of virgins to test their sexual response). A final reason for sampling is its greater accuracy in problems where it is difficult to reach all members of a population—for example, where individuals are widely dispersed or in relatively inaccessible areas. For these reasons, the issue of sampling and making inferences to populations is a major aspect of the scientific method.

REPRESENTATIVENESS   Essentially, inference from samples to populations is a matter of the confidence that can be placed in the representativeness of the sample. A sample is representative to the degree to which it reflects the characteristics of a population. For example, if 10 percent of a population is on welfare, the sample should reflect the same percentage.

It must be stressed that the representativeness of a sample is difficult, if not impossible, to check. Often a sample is taken precisely because an estimate is needed on the *unknown* characteristics of the population. Furthermore, some populations are indefinitely large, or nearly so, which defies accurate knowledge about their characteristics. For these reasons, instead of observing the degree to which a sample is representative, researchers rely upon their confidence in the nature of the sampling procedure (a random sample is considered best). Consequently, in the final analysis, the representativeness of a sample is assumed rather than proved.

It is likely that representativeness is to some extent dependent upon the degree of precision to which the population is specified, the adequacy of the sample, and the heterogeneity of the population. Confidence in the representativeness of a sample is increased if the population is well defined—for example, if a list is obtained of the names of all males in the United States or all freshmen in universities.

Adequacy is an important consideration only if a very small sample is taken. To be adequate, a sample must be of sufficient size to allow the researchers to have confidence (according to statistical techniques) in the inference. In studying male sexual potency, we would hardly have confidence if four males in the United States were examined and then a generalization was made to all males in the country; or if we were concerned with quality control for canned peaches, we would not have confidence in selecting one can in ten million as representative of all.

Finally, representativeness depends on the degree of homogeneity of the population. The more alike the units of the population, the smaller the sample can be and still be representative. Compare, for example, taking a sample from a barrel of oil with taking a sample of all the males in the United States. In a chemical laboratory, only a drop of oil is required to analyze the chemical components of the whole barrel.

To increase the chances of obtaining representativeness, a *random* probability sample should be selected from a population. In a random sample, each unit has an equal chance of being chosen, and the selection of any one unit has no effect on the selection of any other. One technique for obtaining a random sample is to take all names of students in an introductory sociology course, place these names on separate pieces of paper and put them into a bowl, mix thoroughly, and blindly select twenty of the slips of paper. Technically, the chosen slip of paper should be replaced into the bowl before the next slip is selected.

Although a random sampling procedure controls for certain types of bias, it does not eliminate error. Sampling error is a major source of unrepresentativeness. For example, it is logically possible (but extremely unlikely) to take a 1 percent sample of adults in the United States and not select anyone over the age of eighty. Since every individual has an equal chance of being chosen, it is also possible to select all males in the sample. This possibility is so remote that it is nearly nonexistent, but the point is that, even with the best sampling procedures, chance produces some error.

SAMPLING BIAS   If a random procedure is not employed, the potential bias of a sample (that is, the degree of unrepresentativeness) is more extensive than is bias from sampling error. For example, in taking some public opinion polls, interviewers are instructed to find a certain percentage of blacks and whites; or Protestants, Catholics, and Jews; or upper-, middle-, and lower-class individuals. Some interviewers, however, will not go to the toughest lower-class neighborhoods for potential interviewees, nor will they go to the most blighted part of the slums. Consequently, since the extremely poor have little chance of entering the sample, the heterogeneity of the population is not completely represented. With a random sample, however, all names of individuals from all classes have an equal chance of being selected, thus minimizing potential bias.

The poll technique should be differentiated from the stratified random sample, where populations also are first divided into categories (such as upper, middle, and lower classes). Unlike the poll, the next step in stratified random sampling is to take random samples of each category or stratum. There are at least two reasons for selecting a stratified random sample over a simple random sample. First, it ensures that a theoretically important variable will be sufficiently represented in the sample. For example, it permits *oversampling* of numerically small categories, which yields a greater number of cases for analysis (e.g., if few Jews are in the population, by stratifying on religion, 90 percent of them can be selected). Second, a stratified random sample increases the homogeneity of the sampled strata, because individuals in each category are alike on the variable selected for stratifying; e.g., all are Jews or are rich.

An example of a rather complex random sample is that used in the Bowerman and Elder study. They took a random sample of a larger sample (selected in the course of another research project) of 19,200 white adolescents from unbroken homes. The larger sample consisted of individuals from the school system (public and parochial) in central Ohio and public schools only in the central region of North Carolina. The resulting data used by Bowerman and Elder represented a 40 percent sample of seventh to ninth grades and a 60 percent sample of tenth to twelfth grades.

MULTISTAGE SAMPLING   To obtain a representative sample, an accurate, up-to-date list of all elements or names in the population is essential; however, population lists usually are nonexistent, incomplete, or out of date. A list of all citizens of the United States simply does not exist, and lists of smaller populations, such as those in telephone directories or automobile registrations, obviously are biased toward those in more economically advantaged positions. Furthermore, as soon as any list is published, and perhaps even before publication, the list becomes at least partially out of date. People are born, die, move, get new telephones, buy new cars, etc. Although no list is perfect, as a general rule, the smaller the population, the more likely it is that a list of its members exists and the more accurate the list is likely to be. To take advantage of this fact, multistage area sampling is often employed by the U.S. Census Bureau, among other such groups.

Briefly, to employ this sample design, samples of areas are usually taken first, and then perhaps samples are taken of individuals within areas. To illustrate (although not following the technique of the U.S. Census Bureau), in order to take a sample of the population of the United States, a random sample of states may be taken first. Within states, a random sample (say, 20 percent) of counties is selected, and then a random sample of districts or blocks within the selected counties is taken. Finally, at the district or block level, adequate lists of the population may exist, and a random sample of these lists can be taken. Although multistage sampling presents a variety of problems, it has proved to be fairly accurate and an adequate way of handling the problem of poor population lists. It also offers the advantages of being a somewhat cheaper method to run than are some other methods, and it facilitates data collection.

ADVANTAGES OF RANDOM SAMPLING   Regardless of the type of random sampling, its use of probability yields two major advantages over nonrandom sampling techniques. First, a probability (random) sample helps control for the researcher's biases. These biases make the sample unrepresentative of the population. We can control such biases, within limits, by selecting the members of the sample purely on the basis of probability, which ensures that each member of the population has an equal chance of being selected. Since each member has an equal chance of being in the sample, biases are avoided that may result from researchers not wanting to interview members of certain races, wanting to avoid slums, or not including someone because he is not at home.

The second advantage of the random sampling technique is that it enables us to state numerically the degree of confidence we have in inferring to the population. A precise notion of the degree of confidence allows one study to be compared with the next. The data in diverse studies therefore are reduced to a comprehensible and comparative form. One consequence of this numerical manipulation is that we can assess the relative merit of two studies.

NONRANDOM SAMPLING TECHNIQUES   Researchers studying disaster areas have little time to specify all individuals in the population and then select a random sample for interviewing. In severe disasters (earthquakes, hurricanes, fires), we hardly know who has survived, and large-scale disorder hampers any systematic inquiry. With such populations, researchers generally must interview those they are able to grab in any way possible. If a population cannot be specified precisely, a random sampling procedure cannot be used.

Five nonrandom (nonprobability) sampling techniques that may be necessary for certain types of research are (1) quota, (2) interval, (3) judgment, (4) systematic, and (5) snowball. Nonrandom sampling procedures are highly suspect because their degree of representativeness cannot be determined with any precision.

In quota sampling, the population is divided into groups according to selected characteristics, for example, high-, medium-, and low-income categories or male and female categories. These characteristics are assumed to be important to the study. In marital happiness studies, it is important to separate husbands from wives, the old from the young, and the wealthy from the poor. Once the important characteristics are determined, a percentage of individuals (a quota) from each category is selected as part of the sample, for example, 5 percent of the husbands and 5 percent of the wives, or 30 percent of the wealthy and 20 percent of the poor. The interviewer is required to make the final selection of individuals within the designated categories.

Interval sampling requires the selection of units or individuals in a periodic sequence. For example, in a study of characteristics of individuals entering a mental hospital, everyone entering on the fifth of each month may be selected, or on some other time-relevant sequence. This technique permits an assessment of changes in individuals over time. We may find that either more or fewer females or more or fewer youths enter the hospital over a given period.

If the researcher has a large amount of experience or knowledge of a problem and a population, a sample may be selected on judgment alone. Such judgmental samples may be used by researchers who truly know which types of people are typical of the population in question. A psychiatrist perhaps can pick out a few typical schizophrenics or manic-depressives, and an expert in gang delinquency can select a few representative lower- and middle-class gangs.

Systematic sampling usually is used with large population lists such as telephone directories. Instead of taking a random sampling of names from the list (where all individuals have an equal chance of being selected), every nth name is chosen (for example, every fifth name or every thirtieth name). Sometimes the first name chosen is based on a random procedure, but once a starting point is established the criterion for selection is followed (every fifth name or some other). The results of a systematic sampling usually are close to those obtained from strict random sampling. There are, however, potential biases in some problems. Alphabetical lists concentrate certain types of names (for example, Irish names like O'Leary, O'Brian, etc., with husband and wife listed separately). It is probable that each individual in a concentrated space is not equally likely to be selected.

Systematic sampling can create bias if lists are ordered from high to low or low to high on an important characteristic. If the population lists individuals from high to low incomes, where one starts will largely determine the average income of the sample. If a list has a cyclical characteristic, a bias results. To illustrate, let us suppose a neighborhood was laid out logically so that every tenth house was on the corner. If we select every tenth house in our sample, we may get the largest houses in the neighborhood and the largest lots. It could prove quite erroneous to generalize any of our results on corner houses to all houses in the neighborhood.

The snowballing technique involves two or more stages,

or steps, of sampling. If we wanted to know who were the most powerful persons in a community, in stage 1 we could ask all board members of the three largest organizations to provide such a list. In stage 2, each of the individuals mentioned (on the list from responses in stage 1) could be asked for the same information. We are likely to get a larger list of names. This procedure can be repeated until the researcher is satisfied that all powerful individuals have been mentioned. The list of names "snowballs," or grows, as we proceed from one stage to the next.

AN EVALUATION OF VOTING BEHAVIOR SAMPLES   Some of the problems and uses of sampling are illustrated by evaluating some voting behavior studies. In the past, certain opinion polls have resulted in large inaccuracies. Perhaps the most famous example is the Literary Digest Poll of over two million persons that predicted, in 1936, a landslide victory for Alf Landon over Franklin D. Roosevelt. Of course, the 1936 presidential election overwhelmingly favored Roosevelt. The poll erred by approximately 20 percentage points. The biases in the Literary Digest Poll led to the inaccurate prediction. Among the more flagrant biases were that (1) only Literary Digest and telephone subscribers were polled (which was biased toward the wealthier and more conservative elements of the population) and (2) only a small percentage of those polled returned the mailed questionnaire (those who did not return the questionnaire may have been those least interested in the election or in a Republican victory). The inaccuracies of the poll illustrate dramatically the importance of both the population sampled and the method of observation (in this case, mailed questionnaires).

A second instance occurred in 1948 when polls by Gallup and others also forecast the wrong winner of a presidential election. Some polls showed that Harry S. Truman would receive less than 45 percent of the popular vote, when in actuality he received about 50 percent and, of course, won the election.

The presidential election polls for 1948 illustrate some of the major problems with *quota sampling* techniques. Quota sampling is based on the premise that we know what the correct variables are. For example, income and religion are related to voting. Therefore, in sampling people to determine how they will vote, we stratify on these variables—that is, we get a percentage of people who are rich and poor and who are Catholic, Protestant, and Jewish. It is quite probable that if we knew the correct variables (related to voting behavior) we probably would not need any polls in order to predict the outcome of elections. All we would need to do is establish the distribution of the variables in the population. For example, if social class is perfectly related to voting behavior, then knowledge of the exact number of voting persons in each class would predict the results. We usually do not, however, know the distribution of many variables in the population that are thought to be predictive. Further, as mentioned earlier, interviewers, in filling their quotas, produce bias by the respondents they select. Too few of the persons interviewed come from the highest and lowest income groups and from the lowest educational groups. Finally, if a trend analysis had been made of the 1948 election polls, it could have been seen that Truman was gaining on Dewey as the election date approached.

Even with a representative and adequate sample, there may be crucial problems of interpretation. Consider, for example, the 1966 contest for governor of California between Ronald Reagan and Edmund G. Brown. The polls did forecast accurately the Reagan victory; however, few polls came anywhere near predicting the large margin of victory by the Republican candidate. Polls generally gave Reagan a margin of victory between 400,000 and 600,000; the election results gave Reagan a margin of victory of nearly 1 1/2 million votes.

The inadequacies of these polls are to be seen not so much in their design (many of them used probability sampling) as in their interpretation. First, election polls generally do not indicate who will turn out to vote, but only how people would vote if they did turn out. Second, many people may say they are undecided in the polls, but will vote for a candidate at election time. To interpret the polls accurately, some indication must be given of how the undecided will vote.

summary

Because of lack of accessibility, limited time, or prohibitive cost, some populations cannot be studied unless they are sampled. The purpose of a sample is to have a basis for making accurate statements about the population.

Samples should be representative. A representative sample reflects the characteristics of the population that are crucial to the researcher. Representativeness is partially dependent upon the degree of precision to which the population is specified, the adequacy of the sample, and the heterogeneity of the population. An adequate sample is of sufficient size to allow researchers to have confidence (according to statistical techniques) that the characteristics of the sample are "true" for the population. The more homogeneous the population, the smaller the sample can be and still be adequate and representative.

The two basic types of sampling procedures are random and nonrandom. Random sampling assures that each individual has an equal chance of being chosen, and the selection of any one individual has no effect on the selection of any other. It is preferred over nonrandom procedures because it helps control for certain biases (leading to unrepresentativeness), and it enables us to establish statistically the degree of confidence in our inferences to the population.

references

Blalock, Hubert M. 1970. *Social Statistics.* 2nd ed. New York: McGraw-Hill Book Company.

Goode, William J., and Paul K. Hatt. 1952. *Methods of Social Research.* New York: McGraw-Hill Book Company. Chapter 14.

Mueller, John H., Karl F. Schuessler, and Herbert Costner. 1970. *Statistical Reasoning in Sociology.* 2nd ed. Boston: Houghton Mifflin Company.

Chapter 4

Research Design

A *research design* designates the logical manner in which individuals or other units are compared and analyzed; it is the basis for making interpretations from the data. The purpose of a design is to ensure a comparison that is not subject to alternative interpretations. Merely knowing that urbanization and technology are related is not enough to justify an interpretation that one causes the other. A third factor—perhaps natural resources or the achievement motivation of a significant percentage of the population—may cause both variables to change together; or the relation may be interpreted in terms of mutual influence (urbanization initially may stimulate advances in technology, and these advances, in turn, may stimulate further urbaniza-

tion). An adequate design will rule out these alternative interpretations. It should be made clear that no design results in
absolute certainty that only one interpretation is possible, although some designs have fewer alternative interpretations than
others.

criteria for design evaluation

Basically, research designs can be evaluated according to four
criteria:

1. Can equality between experimental and control
   groups be pretested (spatial control)?
2. Can extraneous factors occurring between the pretests and posttests be controlled (temporal control)?
3. Does the design permit an analysis of the pretest
   and posttest individual scores (analysis of changes)?
4. Is the design representative in terms of sampling of
   units and the utilization of uncontrived or realistic
   situations that adequately reflect the environment in
   question (representativeness)?

SPATIAL AND TEMPORAL CONTROL   Spatial and temporal
control are achieved by using a control group in the design.
Control groups are usually used only in experiments, and this
design is rare in sociological research. A control group contains
individuals who, ideally, are just like those in the experimental
group, except that they do not receive the experimental conditions or treatment.

With regard to spatial control, there are two ways to
make the experimental and control groups roughly equal in
composition. One way is to *match* individuals on relevant characteristics. For example, for every male in the experimental group
there should be one in the control group; for every upper-class
subject in one group there should be one in the other; and for
every genius in the experimental group there should be one in
the control group. The major drawback in matching (although it

is a fairly precise procedure) is that there may be many known and unknown variables that are relevant to the study, but only upon a few of the variables can groups be adequately equated in any experimental situation.

To counteract this, *randomization* (random assignment) is often used. Randomization is the procedure by which subjects are assigned to experimental groups and control groups on a probabilistic basis. That is, by assigning subjects randomly to the two groups, the effects of unknown and known variables are, within probability limits, equally distributed. Consequently, within limits, their effects balance each other out and essentially are controlled. An example of randomization is to take one hundred subjects and, by flipping a coin for each subject, divide them into two groups, experimental and control. The basic technique for checking the initial similarity of both groups is by a pretest, which measures all individuals on selected characteristics.

In conducting an experiment, only the experimental group receives the stimulus or treatment (independent or experimental variable). Examples of such stimuli or treatments might be a speech to reduce prejudice, a speed-reading course, tobacco tar rubbed on rats, techniques for learning nonsense syllables, elected versus appointed leaders in small-group studies, etc. The control group is treated identically to the experimental group, except that it does not receive the stimulus. To judge the effects of a movie on attitudes toward the United Nations, for example, the experimental group will look at the movie, while the control group will do nothing or will see a "neutral" movie.

The importance of spatial control is linked to the interpretation of the changes in the experimental group. Consider the following example of a 5-point scale of favorableness toward the United Nations, where the experimental group has a pretest average of 2.5, while the control group has an average of 1.5. In the posttest (after the movie is shown), we discover that the experimental group has an average of 3.5, while the control group has an average of 2.5. Can we say that the difference in posttests between the two groups is due to the movie or simply to the fact that the two groups were different to start with? In this instance, it seems obvious that the movie has *not* had an effect, because without the movie the control-group score changed as much as did the score for the experimental group.

To illustrate the importance of the control group in temporal control (control over extraneous factors), suppose that before seeing a pro–United Nations movie a group is highly prejudiced against the UN, and after the movie the members have favorable attitudes. This change in attitude could be due to the movie, or it could be due to current world events, among other factors. Perhaps the UN had prevented a small tactical war at about the same time the group was shown the movie. How can we determine whether the movie or the recent world event changed the attitudes from anti– to pro–United Nations? Actually, it is a rather simple matter to make this determination if a control is used. If the control group, who did not see the movie, also changed from unfavorable to favorable sentiment toward the UN, then the change could reasonably be attributed to the current world event. If, however, the experimental group did change while the control group did not, it is more reasonable to attribute the effect to the movie (which, ideally, is the only factor differentiating the two groups). Note, however, that if the control group had attitudes that differed to begin with from those of the experimental group, there would be no way of knowing whether the differences between the two groups after the stimulus was administered were due to the stimulus or to the previous difference.

ANALYSIS OF CHANGES   Analysis of changes refers to the analysis of the differences in individual scores or responses between the pretest and the posttest, rather than to the observation of the overall rate or average for the group. Consider again the example of the pro–United Nations movie. In trying to determine the influence of the movie, assume we have determined the anti– or pro–United Nations pretest scores for a sample of one hundred subjects. Suppose, as before, these scores range along a continuum from 1 (anti–United Nations) to 5 (pro–United Nations). After the movie the subjects in the sample are again given questionnaires that determine attitudes toward the United Nations. Suppose that the mean score is 2.5 before the movie (slightly anti) and 3.5 after the movie (slightly pro). This indicates that the movie has had an effect in causing persons to become more favorably oriented toward the United Nations (if there are no temporal or spatial control factors to confound the issue). We assume, at this point, that each individual in the sample shows an increase in his attitude score (more favorable) from pretest to posttest. Individuals with a pretest score of 1 should have a posttest score of 2; those with a pretest score of 2 should have a posttest score of 3, and so on. Those with a pretest score of 5, of course, should remain the same.

Suppose, however, that the actual distribution of pretest and posttest scores is as shown in Table 3. Let us also suppose that the distribution is consistent with the change in mean score from 2.5 to 3.5. Note that there are two distinct sets in terms of response patterns. In general, those with pretest scores of 1, 2, and 3 became more favorably disposed toward the United Nations, although some jumped as high as 4 points and others only 1 or not at all. On the other hand, those who were favorably disposed toward the United Nations (pretest scores of 4 or 5) experienced a decrease in scores, indicating that the movie may have had an adverse effect on them.

The hypothetical movie had an effect on practically all respondents, but largely in conjunction with pretest attitudes.

TABLE 3. *Joint distribution of the pretest and posttest scores of 100 hypothetical respondents*

Pretest Scores	1	2	3	4	5
Total Respondents	20	40	20	10	10
Posttest Scores					
5	5	10	5	0	0
4	10	10	10	0	0
3	5	20	5	5	0
2	0	0	0	5	5
1	0	0	0	0	5

That is, the movie *interacted* with preexisting attitudes to produce an effect. Persons with an unfavorable attitude became more favorably disposed, while those with a favorable attitude became less favorably disposed. Such an interaction effect could not be found without an analysis of changes between pretest and posttest scores.

REPRESENTATIVENESS   The final criterion listed in judging a research design is representativeness, which refers to sampling and to the utilization of realistic situations. In general, representativeness, in terms of sampling, requires one of the types of random procedure discussed previously. A random sample enables us to infer to the population from the knowledge of the data obtained from the part actually studied.

The importance of realistic or natural settings, as opposed to contrived designs such as in a laboratory experiment, is a debatable point. The debate centers around the argument that people placed in "unreal" situations, such as in problem-solving experiments in a laboratory, do not behave in the same way as they do in their everyday-life activities. If people emerge as leaders in a small experimental group, will they also emerge as leaders in their home communities? It is probable that some experiments can be generalized to the natural environment, while others cannot. It should be noted, however, that scientific laws are general and may apply to many different kinds of situations. Moreover, even contrived experimental settings are "real" to the subjects.

the variety of research designs

Perhaps the advantages and limitations of the various designs can best be illustrated by first presenting the simplest design and then progressively adding elements until the classical randomized experiment is reached.

THE CASE STUDY   The one-shot case study (although technically not a design because it does not involve a comparison) involves the observation of one population or sample at one point in time. The major purpose of this design is to describe a unit, rather than to test hypotheses. For example, the case study may involve the investigation of a large business enterprise, an urbanized area, or a community organization. Suppose it is found in the business enterprise that most of the employees favor a wage-investment plan in company stock. Suppose, further, that the company had just gone through an extensive advertising campaign about the benefits of owning its stock. Can we assume that the advertising campaign was effective in making employees favorably disposed to investing in company stock? This type of question cannot be answered with a case study or survey at one point in time because (1) there is no way of knowing whether employees were favorably disposed before the advertising campaign, and (2) there is no control over other possible factors that may have influenced employee attitudes on this issue.

SURVEY DESIGNS   Two survey designs that are often used in the study of social phenomena (and are not experimental) are labeled the *correlational study* and the *panel design*. The correlational study compares two or more units at one point in time. To illustrate, two countries may be compared with respect to level of technology and industrial or occupational division of labor; or Boy Scouts and matched nonmembers may be compared in terms of the marital happiness of the boys' parents. This design is used extensively in sociological study, but the findings should be interpreted with caution because a control group is not used. It does not, therefore, control for the effects of extraneous factors that may be the causes of the differences between the two groups. As a substitute for control by design (as in experiments), social researchers often employ statistical control techniques such as partialling, partial correlation, and standardization. These techniques are discussed in the chapter on data analysis.

The panel design is often referred to as the social design par excellence because (1) it is used in natural settings, (2) it is the only design that yields a study of social process (temporal sequence of events or individual changes), (3) as a nonexperimental technique, it isolates the time priority of variables (determines which ones change first), and (4) it yields a large body of information about respondents. A panel design may be defined as repeated observations on the same sample over a period of time. It is differentiated from the classical randomized experiment by the fact that there is no control over the experimental variable.

To assess whether or not employees previously favored company stock, a panel is necessary because pretest and posttest attitudinal scores can be obtained for each individual. With pretest and posttest scores it can be determined readily if attitudes became more favorably disposed after the advertising campaign was conducted. The question, however, of whether other factors have influenced attitudes cannot be answered by a pretest.

Since repeated measurements are made on the same group, an enormous body of information can be accumulated by asking a few different questions each time, and the changes in characteristics over a period of time can be measured. Furthermore, in such longitudinal studies, the events that lead to a change in attitude or behavior can generally be established, which provides a time priority among variables. For example, in an election campaign the effectiveness of a speech by a presidential candidate can be assessed by finding out who listened to the speech and, of these, which ones changed their opinions, their party loyalties, the candidate for whom they planned to vote, etc. Since we know how the respondents felt before the speech, we need not conjecture about the change—we measure it. Moreover, since the political speech came between two observational periods, it is relatively easy to establish a time sequence. This leads directly into the study of social process or change. By the use of the panel design, longitudinal effects and subsequent social changes can be determined for political campaigns, economic development, technological innovations, urbanization, modifications of the judiciary system, change in governmental leaders, etc.

THE EXPERIMENTAL DESIGN   Suppose, now, that a control group is used and a posttest is given at the same time as the posttest for the experimental group. In this design, not only can we establish whether the experimental group changed to a more favorable attitude toward company stock, but we can see if the experimental group (which was exposed to the advertising campaign) is more favorably disposed than the control group (which was not exposed to the advertising campaign). For illustrative purposes, suppose that on a 10-point scale (with 10 being the most favorable) the experimental group changes from an average score of 3 in the pretest to an average score of 7 in the posttest; and further, that the posttest score for the control group is 5. Can we assume that the advertising campaign had its intended effect? The answer is no, because we do not know what, if anything, has happened to the control group, let alone whether or not the control group was comparable (similar) to the experimental group in the pretest. For example, if the control group changed from a pretest score of 1 to a posttest score of 5 (without the influence of the advertising campaign) they would have equaled the amount of change in the experimental group. Under these conditions we could hardly say that the advertising campaign had any effect at all.

To counteract this possibility, a pretest is needed for the control group. The pretest completes the design for what is often referred to as the *classical randomized experiment* (CRE) or the classical experimental design. In the CRE we can establish (1) the time priority of change, (2) whether or not the experimental group did change in the predicted direction, and (3) whether or not the change was caused by the experimental variable (advertising campaign) or by extraneous variables.

In the designs just discussed, the factors of *history* and *maturation* frequently confound interpretations by producing extraneous variables. With regard to the effect of history, consider the example of buying company stock. During the time of the campaign the company's stock may have substantially increased in value, or the company may have offered an incentive to buy stock by giving lower prices to employees. Needless to say, these historical effects could have caused the change in attitude. With regard to maturation, during the campaign employees grew older (mature), and perhaps there is a relation between age and attitude toward buying stock. If so, whether or not there was a campaign, employees would have become more favorably disposed. The control-group scores allow us to assess the probability of these alternative explanations produced by history and maturation. First, assume that the experimental and control groups each had similar pretest scores of 3. Since the control group is differentiated from the experimental group by not being exposed to the stimulus, in this case the advertising campaign, any difference in the posttest scores between the two groups (within probability limits) can be attributed to the stimulus. For example, if the posttest average for the experimental group is 7, and for the control group it is 5, we can assume that two of the units of change were due to the campaign. On the other hand, since the control group changed from 3 to 5, we can assume that either history or maturation also had an affect on the attitudes of the subjects.

Besides maturation and history effects, there are six other factors that may lead to inaccurate interpretations. First is *instrument decay,* which refers to the observational technique. Springs on scales may lose their tension, and likewise, people may become fatigued in answering long questionnaires, or interviewers and observers may tire and lose some of their discriminatory capabilities. These problems lead to unreliable results, but they may be partially handled by a control group. Presumably, the change in the measuring instrument will affect both experimental and control groups; consequently, the difference between the two groups cannot be attributed to decay of the instrument.

The second factor is *selection,* which refers to the similarity of the groups being compared. People who listen to political speeches are probably different from those who do not. If listeners and nonlisteners are compared to determine the effects of the speech on those who listened, the results may be biased by the fact that the two groups were different in the pretest. The technique of randomization in the classical randomized experiment reduces the effects of biased selection.

Mortality, the third factor, may affect the results even if the two groups compared were the same in the pretest stage. A biased subset of members in either group may somehow drop out of the study. Design mortality refers to members dropping out: actual death, moving away, illness, refusal to take a posttest, etc. Those persons who refuse to take the stimulus (for example, refuse to see a pro–United Nations movie) may be different from those who are willing. Consequently, mortality may change the composition of the experimental group so that it is no longer comparable with the control group.

The fourth factor, statistical *regression,* may bias the results of certain studies. Regression refers to the fact that extreme scores (in either direction) tend to be less extreme in a subsequent period of observation; that is, they move, or regress, toward the mean score. For example, in studies of genetics, if all other factors are held equal, the children of tall parents tend to be slightly shorter than their parents and the children of small parents tend to be slightly taller. As another example, in studying a group with extreme IQ scores, the subjects will have a slightly lower average score on a subsequent test (if we could subtract the effects of learning from the first test). Regression effects are most important in those studies where extreme groups (ends of continuums) are selected for further analysis. We would expect these groups to be less extreme on a subsequent test because of regression effects alone. Suppose a group of individuals with IQ scores of 140 and over are given a speed-reading course that is thought to increase performance on IQ tests. Suppose, further, that the second IQ tests show the same average IQ for the group as did the first pretest set. It quite probably would be wrong to conclude that the speed-reading course had no effect, because the posttest scores may be due, in part, to regression. That is, the effects of regression may have been balanced out by the effects of the speed-reading course.

Fifth, the *sensitization* of subjects—that is, increased awareness of factors that change responses—can lead to substantial bias. Nonsensitization of subjects is often a difficult goal to achieve, but it is extremely crucial in the research design (and to the selection of observational techniques). Individuals selected for a laboratory experiment have been singled out for study and they are aware of it. Some subjects try either to fool or to please the researcher. Either way, they hardly represent a population that is not aware of being studied. In a classic study by F. J. Roethlisberger and W. J. Dickson, subjects in a work group increased their output no matter what innovation was tried, simply because they were singled out for an experiment.[1]

Finally, researchers can bias the responses of subjects independently of the effects of the stimulus, i.e., *experimenter effects* (Robert Rosenthal, 1966). For example, if an experimenter believes he is working with "bright" rats, his rats solve maze problems more quickly than those experimenters who believe they are not working with bright rats. Applied to grade schools, the IQ scores of students thought to be bright by their teachers increase more than IQ scores of those considered to be average or below average. These results are not caused by the actual intelligence of the students, but by the teacher's attitudes and behavior based on the belief that one student is brighter than another.

In response to Rosenthal's study, the awareness of biases by the researcher and the use of standard measuring instruments should reduce experimenter effects; that is, a well-trained researcher and well-conceived research are the best guards against such effects.

A technique for reducing biases due to sensitization and

[1]*Management and the Worker,* Harvard University Press, Cambridge, Mass., 1939.

experimenter effects is the *double blind*. In the double blind neither the subject nor the researcher knows the nature of the experimental variable. Subjects are not told whether they are receiving a new wonder drug or a placebo (an inert substance, often a sugar pill). Records are kept on just who receives the wonder drug and who does not. These records are checked by the researcher after the experiment.

summary

In this summary, designs are restated in terms of three broad conceptual types: experiments, case studies, and surveys (panel, poll, or correlational study). That is, the forms of designs range from the highly controlled laboratory experiment to the loosely structured participant observation or case study. In addition to experiments and case studies, a significant percentage of social research is based on the survey technique. A social survey predominantly involves a rather large sample of a population or some one selected segment and is usually associated with the observational techniques of the questionnaire and interview.

Three short examples should suffice to summarize these general designs. A classic example of the experiment is provided by Muzafer Sherif's autokinetic study (1936). Briefly, subjects were placed in a room that was totally dark except for one pinpoint of light. They were asked to tell in which direction and how far the light moved. Actually, the light was stationary throughout the experiment. If the subjects were alone in the experiment, there was little or no agreement on the movement of the light. When subjects went through the experiment in groups, however, there tended to be high agreement among members on the direction and distance of the light's movement. The experiment rather uniquely illustrated social influence on individual decisions.

The study by Elder (Chapter 2 references) provides an example of the survey design. His study of family structure and educational achievement involved random samples of about one thousand people of eighteen years of age and over in the United States, Great Britain, West Germany, Italy, and Mexico. From interview data, Elder found an inverse (negative) relation between parental dominance in adolescence and the probability of reaching secondary school; that is, as parental dominance increased, the probability of going to secondary school decreased.

Finally, a good example of a case study is William F. Whyte's intensive study of a "street-corner gang." Whyte hung out with members of the gang and participated in many of their activities, such as bowling, pool, cards, drinking, and eating. His analysis included a detailed description of the interrelations between members and the importance of the gang to each participant. One of his major conclusions was that the hierarchical position held by a member of the gang influenced his behavior; for example, bowling scores were positively related to position.

The three designs of experiments, surveys, and case studies have their strengths and weaknesses. An experimental design is characterized by a significant amount of control over the experimental or independent variable and over extraneous factors. That is, in an experiment, the use of a control group, of pretests and posttests, and of the techniques of matching and randomization (to equate the experimental and control groups) reduces the probability of inaccurate interpretation of the results. Experiments, however, can rarely be performed on a large group of people. Consequently, inferences from most experiments are quite limited in scope, and they seldom apply with accuracy to a large population. Moreover, the very act of placing individuals in small, contrived, and sometimes intense situations may actually change the participants so they no longer represent their community. Because of these two factors (a small experimental sample and sensitized subjects), experiments are usually quite low in the degree to which they represent any designated population. The low degree of representativeness, however, is counteracted by the high degree of control, and consequently an accurate interpretation of results can be made.

ease of interpreting results but low degree of representativeness & might not represent community.

Surveys, as compared with experiments, are often characterized by a high degree of representativeness but a low degree of control over extraneous factors. Surveys usually employ a random sampling technique, which yields some confidence of representativeness within specified limits. Because surveys do not have experimental and control groups, however, other factors besides the independent variables may have produced the changes in the dependent variable. Consequently, surveys are low on control over extraneous factors but possess the advantage of being high on representativeness.

Compared with experiments, a case study is low on control, and compared with surveys it is low on representativeness. One can hardly differentiate cause from effect, and inferring from the intensive study of one or a few cases involves a high and generally unknown amount of risk. The major advantage of a case study lies in the richness of its descriptive examples that results from the intensive study of one or a few units. The results of these studies often suggest perceptive hypotheses that subsequently should be tested under experimental and survey situations.

references

Campbell, Donald T., and Julian C. Stanley. 1966. *Experimental and Quasi-Experimental Designs for Research.* Chicago: Rand McNally & Company.

Davis, James A. 1971. *Elementary Survey Analysis.* Englewood Cliffs, New Jersey: Prentice-Hall.

Festinger, Leon, and Daniel Katz (eds.). 1953. *Research Methods in the Social Sciences.* New York: The Dryden Press. Chapters 1, 2, 3, and 4.

Rosenthal, Robert. 1966. *Experimenter Effects in Behavioral Research.* New York: Appleton-Century-Crofts.

Ross, John A., and Perry Smith. 1965. "Designs of the Single-Stimulus, All-or-Nothing Type," *American Sociological Review,* **30:**68–80 (February).

Sherif, Muzafer. 1936. *The Psychology of Social Norms.* New York: Harper & Row, Publishers.

Stouffer, Samuel A. 1950. "Some Observations on Study Design," *American Journal of Sociology,* **5:**355–361 (January).

Warwick, Donald P., and Samuel Osheson (eds.). 1973. *Comparative Research Methods.* Englewood Cliffs, New Jersey: Prentice-Hall.

Whyte, William F. 1955. *Street Corner Society.* 2nd ed. Chicago: University of Chicago Press.

Chapter 5

Methods of
Observation

Observational methods of social phenomena can be divided into three types: (1) those directly eliciting responses from subjects by questioning (questionnaires, schedules, and interview guides); (2) those utilizing either human observers (participant-observers or judges) or mechanical observers (cameras, tape recorders, interaction chronograph, etc.); and (3) physical-trace evidence (e.g., litter and fossils). They can be further classified into primary sources (data gathered and used by the researcher) and secondary sources (data used by the researcher but gathered by someone else—for example, census reports, vital-statistics records, company files, and sales receipts). The variety of observational techniques not only provide a wealth of data for the social sciences, but they also provide validity checks on one another. That is, if different techniques lead to similar conclusions, more confidence can be placed in each technique (and the conclusions) than if each is used alone.

questionnaires, schedules, and interview guides

The three devices used for direct questioning of respondents are highly versatile instruments in that almost any social topic (and a great number of them) can be covered in a single session. Moreover, they have the positive utility of getting immediate data (information obtained from secondary sources is usually older), the exact questions desired can be asked, and the reliability of the data can be assessed.

THE QUESTIONNAIRE   The questionnaire is an instrument comprised of a series of questions that are filled in by the respondent himself. It may be handed out to him at work or school, or it may be mailed to him at home. A mailed questionnaire is a useful technique if respondents are spread out over a fairly large geographical area and the researcher has limited resources (in terms of money and assistance). Having the respondent fill out the questionnaire himself usually saves time and money, but this method has several disadvantages compared with the schedule or interview guide. The major disadvantages are:

1. The population of study is restricted, because respondents must be able at least to read and write.
2. There is a high degree of self-selection, leading to a comparatively low response or return rate—that is,

those most interested or highly educated are most likely to respond.

3. The questionnaire must be restricted in length and scope, because respondents lose interest or become fatigued.

4. There is a lack of depth interviewing (by definition) or probing for the meaning of statements.

The disadvantages of the mailed questionnaire are usually more extreme than are those of direct contact with respondents. For example, the response rates often are quite low (a 30 percent return is not uncommon); an intelligent population (at least a high-school education) is often required; and the questionnaire usually must be extremely short.

The questionnaire, schedule, and interview guide ideally are constructed around a set of related items. That is, they are usually comprised of a set of questions closely related to and reflecting upon the actual problem or problems under study. These questions are either *structured* (the respondent is allowed a limited number of responses) or *unstructured* (open-ended questions are presented to which the respondent gives his own answer). An example of a structured question is to ask the respondent to indicate the sex of a person by checking one of the categories, "male" or "female." An example of an unstructured question is, "What is your opinion on the new morality?" Structured items are more comparable from one person to the next and are generally easier to analyze; however, they limit respondents to preconceived categories that may not exhaust all possibilities or be meaningful or interpretable. Unstructured items allow for probing into meaning, but they usually have a low degree of reliability; that is, repeated questioning of the same respondents may yield different results.

In Bowerman and Elder's study (Chapter 2 references), a questionnaire was used to gather the relevant information. This questionnaire is characterized by a predominance of structured items; and almost all items are concerned with family structural patterns and their effects on the behavior and attitudes of family members. For example, child-rearing practices were measured by asking the following question and allowing the respondent to select one of the answers.

In general, how are most decisions made between you and your (mother/father)?

AUTOCRATIC   *My (mother/father) just tells me what to do.*

AUTHORITARIAN   *(Mother/Father) listens to me, but makes the decision (herself/himself).*

DEMOCRATIC   *I have considerable opportunity to make my own decisions, but my (mother/father) has the final word.*

EQUALITARIAN   *My opinions are as important as my (mother's/father's) in deciding what I should do.*

PERMISSIVE   *I can make my own decisions, but my (mother/father) would like me to consider (her/his) opinion.*

LAISSEZ FAIRE   *I can do what I want, regardless of what my (mother/father) thinks.*

IGNORING   *My (mother/father) doesn't care what I do.*

THE SCHEDULE AND INTERVIEW GUIDE   Both the schedule and the interview guide are comprised of a set of items or questions (structured or unstructured) that are asked and filled in by an interviewer in a face-to-face situation with the respondent. Essentially, a schedule is a questionnaire that is read to the respondents. Compared with the population that is researched through the use of a questionnaire, the population for research relying on an interview schedule is not as restricted (respondents need not read or write, but must merely be able to understand the language of the interviewer), though the sample must usually be restricted in the sense of being much smaller. Also, the interview may be longer, since the interviewer acts as a stimulant to the respondent. Furthermore, the meanings of troublesome questions can be explained to respondents, and interviewers can probe deeply into any question. Finally, the schedule usually elicits a higher response rate than does the questionnaire.

The interview guide is actually a loosely structured schedule. It merely lists the topics an interviewer has been instructed to cover. Consequently, all questions are unstructured, which does not lead to comparability in the wording of questions from one respondent to another. It does, however, provide flexibility in the manner, order, and language of the questions. This technique is useful in a preliminary study (such as a pretest or pilot study) where the results can lead to more structured questions for the actual study. Moreover, the guide may be the only effective technique for studying areas or topics in which little is known. A more structured instrument would be premature and useless. As a general rule, the more known about a particular area, the more structured the items can be and still yield meaningful answers.

The schedule, guide, and questionnaire are beset by six problems that may lead to unreliable results. These problems are:

1. Sensitized subjects who respond differently because of the presence of an interviewer or simply because they are being questioned, which means that results cannot be inferred to a population.
2. Faulty memory of subjects.
3. A response rate that is almost always less than 100 percent (people refuse to answer, die, move away, or just cannot be found), which usually indicates a self-selection bias of, perhaps, a known direction, but to an unknown degree; for example, for those who respond, the more highly educated usually are

overrepresented and the lower-income groups are underrepresented.
4. The tendency of the questions to tap opinions, attitudes, or perceived behavior, but seldom actual behavior that may be crucial to certain problems.
5. Respondents who are unqualified for providing certain kinds of data; e.g., they may not have the training to say whether or not they are paranoid, have cancer, or are prejudiced.
6. Invalid responses owing to subjects lying, giving responses that they feel the researcher wants, or giving answers that represent their community or group rather than themselves.

Even though formidable, these problems may not be as serious as the list seems to suggest. For example, (1) indirect measures or undetected observations may be used if subjects are easily sensitized by direct questioning; (2) on many topics, few respondents lie; (3) a follow-up sample may be taken to determine selection bias; and (4) if respondents are unqualified to answer certain questions, consultation with "experts" may provide the necessary information.

Because of the above problems, however, several studies have resorted to using human observers (other than respondents), mechanical devices, and physical-trace evidence. These techniques, for the most part, are concerned with actual rather than perceived behavior.

human observers

Observers usually come under the labels of *judges* or *participants.* A judge is an observer who is detached (nonparticipant) from the situation and uses a fairly rigid set of predetermined categories to code events. Judges are confined to contests, direct observation of groups and individuals, and coding of either verbal responses or actual behavior. The judge's task (which may or may not involve structured items) is to rank (classify) contestants with regard to some criteria, such as beauty or personality, or to classify attitudes or behavior into separate categories. The resulting rank orders or classification schemes are subsequently used for both descriptive and inference purposes. For example, Robert F. Bales (1950) developed twelve well-defined categories of interaction for the observation of small groups in interaction. The twelve categories are:

1. Shows solidarity
2. Shows tension release
3. Agrees
4. Gives suggestion
5. Gives opinion
6. Gives orientation
7. Asks for orientation
8. Asks for opinion
9. Asks for suggestion
10. Disagrees
11. Shows tension
12. Shows antagonism

His judges, using a moving graph, may sit behind a one-way mirror and record the behavior of the group members in terms of these twelve categories.

Participant-observers are involved in the social setting while recording events. This usually is referred to as participant observation. Not only does the researcher participate to some extent in his own study, but he also gathers data about the individuals in his sample or universe. There is a wide variation in the degree of participation of the observer. Minimum participation may lead the researcher to take a distant-observer role, trying not to get too close to the respondents or to influence them in any way. For example, to study a small work group in a business enterprise, the observer may tell the group he is a social scientist who wants to observe the proceedings from the back of the room. The work group, it is hoped, will proceed as usual, and the researcher will interact with them as little as possible. At the other extreme, the researcher may take one of the group's roles as a vantage point for observation. He may, to illustrate, become an inmate in a prison or, as an anthropologist, take an active part in the ceremonies of one of the peoples he is investigating. Whether minimally or extensively involved in the setting, the researcher is always in danger of influencing the group by his presence or of being influenced by the group and losing his detachment and objectivity.

The major purpose of participant observation is exploratory. In societies, large-scale organizations, or small groups where relatively little is known, this method is useful for exploring the structural and psychological makeup of groups and individuals, and for forming tentative hypotheses that may be formally tested with another technique.

Participant observation, however, also may be used to test hypotheses if reliability (repeated observations yield similar results) can be introduced into the technique. Employing systematic rather than random observations, with formal rules stating how and what is to be observed and recorded (and how to analyze the observation records), may lead to reliable results. For example, checking the consistency of observations between two or more observers is a useful technique for establishing confidence in the data.

There are at least five major problems associated with participant observation. The first problem is the lack of reliability resulting from random observations by the researcher. It is not likely that two separate observers will perceive and record the same events in the same way. As stated above, however, observations may become at least somewhat systematic by establishing formal procedures that are followed in the field. Unreliability comes from selective perception on the part of observers. Given a specified theory or a particular interest or training, observers are likely to perceive and record different events or to interpret them in different ways. The second problem is that the participant-observer may sensitize subjects by his presence, thus altering their behavior and, consequently, not getting the true picture. Third, the actual role taken by the observer narrows his range of experience. For example, a teller in the bank can hardly go to the bank president for personal information. Fourth, the observer may become so involved in the group that he loses objectivity. Finally, most observers must wait passively for occurrences. In fact, it is possible that particular events in which they are most interested may not occur in the time span during which they are observing.

These factors are counteracted by five advantages of participant observation. First, the observations take place in a "natural" setting, so the only contrived aspect is the observer himself. Second, the observer is able to perceive the emotional reactions of his subjects, which may lead to fruitful hypotheses. Third, by observing over an extended period of time, a great deal of information can be obtained. Although questionnaires and interviews are more efficient data-gathering techniques and can provide an enormous amount of information, their extensiveness is limited by the subject's fatigue or boredom. A fourth factor is that the observer is able to record the context, which gives meaning to the respondent's expressions of opinions and values. Finally, if the observer can establish solid relations (rapport), he may be able to ask sensitive questions that would otherwise not be permissible.

Human observers can make extensive use of indicators of behavioral phenomena. For example, a rather obvious indicator of the success of the evangelist Billy Graham occurred in New York when several participant-observers (conducting a study of Graham's techniques and audience reaction) became totally involved participants and walked down the aisle themselves. The effectiveness of horror or ghost stories told to a group of children can be indicated by the size of the circle at the beginning of the story and at the end. Do the children huddle closer together by the scariness of the stories? If you want to know how far a group of social-protest demonstrators are expecting to go, note whether the women are wearing dresses or pants. Wearing pants is an indicator that they feel it is likely they are going to spend the night in jail. Calluses are often observable indicators of certain classes of activities or occupations. Finally, pupil dilation may indicate fear, as suggested by Charles Darwin; interest on the part of clients, as interpreted by Chinese jade dealers; or a recent fix, in the case of junkies.

mechanical devices

Because people are selective and imprecise in the recording of events, mechanical recording devices are important for certain types of social research. Individuals make observational errors, recording errors, tabulating errors, and furthermore, they may be unsure of how to classify an event. Moreover, as stated previously, observers are selectively biased in what and how they observe so that important factors may be missed altogether. Finally, unaided by measuring tools (for example, a ruler or scale), persons can give only rather gross information, such as saying a boy is tall or heavy. They are not able to say how tall or how heavy. These arguments strongly argue for mechanical devices either to aid the human observer or to do the observing for him.

The most commonly used mechanical devices in the social sciences are audio and visual tape recordings, moving-picture and still cameras, the interaction chronograph (which measures direction and frequency of interaction), and Robert F. Bales' interaction machine. The data provided by these instruments can be analyzed long after the events have occurred. Pictures and tape recordings tend also to give a more complete description of events than do observers' notes. An advantage of certain mechanical devices, such as tape recordings or movies, is that they frequently contain more information than is required for a specific research problem. Consequently, they can provide a great deal of data for secondary analysis. For example, inflections or loudness of voices in tape recordings may be completely ignored by the initial researcher but may become the crucial variables in another study in which the data are used as a secondary source.

Some mechanical devices, such as the microsc
the telescope, permit observations that are otherwise no
ble. Other devices may be used as rather precise measuring
instruments. Obvious examples are weighing scales, rulers,
electrocardiographs, and watches. In the social sciences, Bales'
interaction machine and the interaction chronograph may be
used to measure the frequency of interaction among a group of
individuals, as well as keeping track of the initiator and the
duration of the interaction. These techniques have led to
important studies of group formation and structure, personality
types, and operational measures of cliques, leaders, followers,
and isolates.

physical-trace evidence

Although seldom used in social research, physical traces (erosion
and accretion measures) lead to important bits of information
that can be used in conjunction with other observational techniques, or they can be used alone as measures of social phenomena. Physical traces are rarely reactive measures (that is, measures that sensitize subjects to certain events and opinions), which
is one of the major faults of most other observational techniques
in the social sciences. Consequently, they are extremely important for ascertaining the degree to which the other techniques
have sensitized subjects, as well as being used as direct and
indirect measures in their own right.

Physical-trace evidence can be classified either as *erosion*
or *accretion.* Erosion traces wear away—that is, selectively wear
on some material (often gradually); while accretion traces build
up—that is, deposit materials over a period of time (again, often
gradually). Examples of erosion traces are the wearing away of
tiles at an exhibit, wear on library books (the measurement used
to determine which books are handled most often or which are
actually read when checked out), the carbon-14 dating method,
and the rate at which children wear out shoes as a measure of
activity. To illustrate an accretion measure, modern police

equipment is used to analyze the soil and other deposited materials (blood) on the shoes and clothing of suspects. (Eugene J. Webb et al. state that Forshufvud, a scientist, in 1961 "uncovered the historic murder of Napoleon in 1821 on the basis of arsenic traces in remains of his hair.") Examples of other accretion measures are the archaeological evidence in the remains of pottery and tools; the evidence in garbage-can refuse indicating who are the drinkers, the lovers, or who is on the brink of financial disaster; or the evidence in graffiti and litter.

Two major limitations of physical traces are (1) they usually measure only selected aspects of the phenomenon, and (2) sometimes they are difficult to interpret. The same, however, can be said for other techniques that sensitize subjects. Since different measuring techniques have different biases, used in conjunction they can lend support to each other's findings. To illustrate, Webb et al. state:

> The floor tiles around the hatching-chick exhibit at Chicago's Museum of Science and Industry must be replaced every six weeks. Tiles in other parts of the museum need not be replaced for years. The selective erosion of tiles, indexed by the replacement rate, is a measure of the relative popularity of exhibits.

It could be that the exhibit is not more popular but that people shuffle around this exhibit and, therefore, wear out the tile. Interpreting the physical-trace erosion as popularity might be in error. Suppose, however, that we also asked visitors to the museum to tell us their favorite exhibit and that their responses overwhelmingly favored the hatching-chick exhibit. This response may be in error because (1) this exhibit may be the most easily remembered, since it was the last exhibit on the tour, or perhaps a demonstration exhibit is more easily remembered, or (2) people may lie (they may not want to admit they were bored by the whole exhibit). Both techniques could be in error by interpreting the results as indicating the hatching-chick exhibit as most popular. When we combine the evidence that is consistent, however, more confidence can be placed in the interpretation.

secondary sources

Secondary sources consist of existing documents that were not collected by the investigator, but were used by him. Anything written or on tape or record or on film can be a secondary source. Social scientists often use as secondary sources governmental records, such as census reports, vital statistics, surveys of manufactures, and special surveys (monthly, yearly, decennially) that have been taken.[1] These data often prove useful in change studies, since particular units (in this instance, countries and their political divisions) are generally measured on several characteristics over a period of years. Other secondary sources that have proved useful to the social scientist are the mass media (newspapers, radio and television broadcasts, magazines, journals, and motion pictures); company sales receipts or records concerning retirement, hiring and firing, absenteeism, and turnover; voting records; records of judicial decisions; prison records; written documents (such as the Constitution and *Who's Who in America*); and personal documents (for example, diaries and letters).

A particular method of analyzing secondary sources that has proved to be increasingly useful to sociologists and political scientists (among others) is *content analysis.* Content analysis is the systematic and objective study of messages usually guided by some rationale (for a general discussion of this topic see Holsti, 1969, Chapter 1). This technique can be applied to any type of recorded symbolic communication. It is usually applied to written documents such as personal diaries, letters, newspapers, magazines, books, and government documents.

To do a content analysis the researcher may select certain themes, words, or sentiments expressed in a message. An editorial page of a newspaper may be studied to assess its treatment of local as opposed to national issues. Key words may be specified to aid in the systematic search for commentary on the community and on the nation. Some words that indicate a

[1]For a useful discussion of secondary sources and library usage see Bart and Frankel, 1971, Chapters 2–6.

local concern are "city" and "community." Words indicating a national concern are "federal" and "national." Once the categories or words are selected, a researcher may systematically count each time they are used in the lead editorial. A predominance in the use of city and community over federal and national indicates more concern for local issues.

The selection of categories requires the careful guidance of a sound rationale. If the rationale is poorly conceived, the content analysis may prove to be trivial or invalid. It is conceivable that a newspaper could mention the word community quite frequently but still be nationally oriented.

Secondary sources have great potential for social inquiry because they often cover a wide range of topics for a number of years and because the researcher cannot sensitize his subjects. Nevertheless, they have some special problems. First, many secondary sources are not current so that a picture of the present (actually the immediate past for scientists) is hard to determine with accuracy. Second, secondary sources often were not put together with the researcher's problem in mind, and consequently, he may not find exactly what he wants. Third, at least in the case of public records, their comparability over time usually leaves something to be desired. The labor-force concept employed by the U.S. Census Bureau has gone through serious changes in definition, negating the use of labor-force statistics for some problems and making the conclusions from others highly tenuous. Fourth, written documents are not only selectively deposited (historically, we probably get a more accurate picture of the life of kings than of serfs), but they selectively survive. Even if you can give a monetary reward to a group for all personal letters from, say, husbands in the army, you probably would get some bias in the letters turned in (for example, those that were less personal or less deceitful). Fifth, although the researcher did not sensitize the subjects in the records, someone did collect the data (for the censuses), and that person may have sensitized them. In addition, some people are aware that the document they are writing will be preserved, and this may influence what they write. Finally, secondary sources may be unreliable owing to distortion by biased recorders.

summary

Primary and secondary data sources may be based on the same observational techniques, even though secondary sources are gathered by someone other than the researcher. The basic observational techniques for the social sciences are questionnaires, schedules, interview guides, human observers, mechanical observers, and physical-trace evidence.

The questionnaire, schedule, and guide (the most prevalent data-gathering methods in sociology) directly request and elicit responses from subjects by questioning. They are particularly adapted to many research problems of a social and social-psychological nature and are highly versatile (that is, they can be used for a variety of topics). Questionnaires are filled in by the respondent, while the schedule and guide are administered by an interviewer. Further, the schedule is more rigidly structured than the guide.

Human observers are either judges or participants. Judges are used in contests, direct observation of individuals and groups, and coding. They are relatively detached from the research setting and use a fairly rigid set of predetermined categories to code events. Participant-observers are involved in the situation while recording events. The degree of participation may be minimal (distant-observer role) or extensive (the observer occupying a major position in a group). Participant observation may be used for exploratory purposes or to test hypotheses. If hypothesis testing is desired, systematic rather than random observations are required for reliability.

Mechanical devices help reduce human error in observation. Commonly used instruments in social research are audio and visual tape recordings, moving-picture and still cameras, and interaction machines. These techniques not only permit observations that otherwise may not be possible, but they also add precision in the measuring of events.

Physical-trace evidence may take the form of accretion (building up) or erosion (wearing away) measures. They may lead to important information in their own right, as well as providing a check on the validity of other observational techniques.

These different observational techniques provide a wealth of data for the social sciences in many areas of interest. Moreover, if used in conjunction with one another, they can increase the confidence placed in any one technique and in the data. The techniques selected depend upon the nature of the problem in question, the sample, the research design, and the available resources (money and assistance), among other factors.

references

Babbie, Earl R. 1973. *Survey Research Methods.* Belmont, California: Wadsworth Publishing Company.

Bales, Robert F. 1950. *Interaction Process Analysis.* Reading, Mass.: Addison-Wesley Publishing Company, Inc.

Bart, Pauline, and Linda Frankel. 1971. *The Student Sociologist's Handbook.* Cambridge, Mass.: Schenkman.

Glazer, Myron. 1972. *The Research Adventure.* New York: Random House.

Gordon, Raymond L. 1975. *Interviewing: Strategy, Techniques, and Tactics.* Revised Edition. Homewood, Illinois: Dorsey Press.

Holsti, Ole R. 1969. *Content Analysis for the Social Sciences and Humanities.* Reading, Mass.: Addison-Wesley Publishing Company, Inc.

Hyman, Herbert H. 1972. *Secondary Analysis of Sample Surveys: Principles, Procedures, and Potentialities.* New York: John Wiley.

Riley, Matilda White. 1963. *Sociological Research.* New York: Harcourt, Brace & World, Inc. Units 1 through 5.

Webb, Eugene J., et al. 1966. *Unobtrusive Measures: Nonreactive Research in the Social Sciences.* Chicago: Rand McNally & Company.

Chapter 6

Data Analysis

Data have meaning only in terms of the interpretations made by the researcher. Frequently, social researchers have a large amount of data that must be "reduced" to some statistical measures before meaningful interpretations can be made. To have on file the age of every person in the United States is an enormous amount of information, but it is incomprehensible in its raw form. Such data are useful only when the average age is specified or relevant age categories are used (e.g., those of school age, the working population, and the aged).

Data reduction consists of grouping information into a few categories or of computing a small number of statistics to adequately describe the characteristics of the sample or population. These few statistics are used to communicate the results of the study and to indicate the comparability of one study with another. Such statistics are either descriptive or inferential.

Descriptive statistics are computed to determine the characteristics of the data at hand. They can be actual numbers, percentages, averages, or measures of spread or relations. As the name implies, they are used to describe the information the researcher has gathered—the numerical data he actually has in hand.

Inference statistics are used to go beyond the data at hand to the universe from which it was drawn—in other words, to estimate the characteristics of the population from which the sample was drawn. For example, if the mean number of criminal acts committed by a random sample of college sophomores in the United States is 2.3, the problem is to estimate the corresponding mean number of criminal acts for the total population of sophomores. These estimations are based on probability statements, so that population characteristics can be specified with reasonable accuracy.

There are two basic definitions of statistics. First, "statistics" is often used as synonymous with "numbers": the actual data gathered and manipulated. For example, the number of unemployed males, the average size of families in Central America, or the average frequency of sexual activity among American undergraduates are all statistics in this sense. This is the popular use of the term. When a newspaper article says, "Statistics have shown that illiteracy has not decreased in the United States," the term refers to numbers. The second meaning of statistics is in terms of the theories and techniques (both descriptive and inferential) that have been developed to manipulate data. In this sense, statistics refers not to the marriage rate for the United States, but to the technique used to obtain the rate. Under this definition, percentages, averages, dispersions, relations, and tests of hypotheses are statistics.

No matter how statistics is defined, it always refers to the manipulation of numerals. In fact, statistics may be looked at, in part, as a belief that certain phenomena (social and physical) can be expressed in numbers in some meaningful way.

descriptive statistics

The way in which variables are measured partially determines the types of statistics that are useful for data analysis. Moreover, measurement is a necessary condition for statistical analysis.

Measurement can be both quantitative and qualitative. Variables are measured quantitatively if they vary in magnitude (greater or smaller amounts), such as in height, weight, population size, IQ, or education. Quantitative measurement occurs by (1) direct enumeration, where the item itself is counted (for example, counting the number of persons in an area); (2) the use of a standard unit by which objects are measured (the foot, the hour, the pound, the acre, etc.); (3) using a "behavioral equivalent" or index that is a measurable indicator of social phenomena (for example, measuring group cohesion by the number of members who attend meetings and measuring marital happiness by the frequency of arguments); and (4) ranking a series of objects. The fourth measurement results in a rank order, where classes can be distinguished from one another in terms of greater or less, although the amount of difference between ranks is unknown. Examples are the scratch test in determining the hardness of minerals, the rank order of contestants, and subjective measures of social class.

Qualitative measurement involves distinguishing one class of objects from another, differentiating not in magnitude but in quality or kind. One may distinguish males from females, Protestants from members of other religious groups, or blondes from brunettes. In this kind of measurement there is no underlying "more" or "less" of some dimension. The items in each category can be counted, but the categories themselves cannot be ordered or ranked.

FREQUENCY DISTRIBUTIONS A frequency distribution is the separation of a variable into mutually exclusive classes and the number of individuals in each class. No matter how variables are measured, if they are operationalized, frequency distributions can be computed for them. A frequency distribution is an important statistical technique because it is (1) the basis for the computation of many other statistics, and (2) an extremely useful descriptive device in its own right. Without such a distribution, data analysis would be limited to impressionistic accounts, which is hardly a basis for reliable and comparative research.

A frequency distribution is used to summarize (usually) a number of observations; consequently, it is a means for useful data reduction. If set up adequately, it provides a neat, accurate, and orderly summary of data that is comprehensible to any competent reader. For example, consider the hypothetical frequency distribution of age to nearest birthday shown in Table 4. It shows that most persons are between eighteen and twenty-one years of age; the most frequent age category is eighteen to nineteen and the least frequent is sixteen to seventeen.

This distribution gives an adequate summary of the ages representing each category. Such frequency distributions are relatively easy to understand and manipulate statistically.

CROSS-CLASSIFICATION So far we have been discussing *univarite* (single variable) frequency distributions (e.g., frequen-

TABLE 4. *Hypothetical frequency distribution of age to nearest birthday*

AGE TO NEAREST BIRTHDAY	FREQUENCY (*f*)				
24–25	111				3
22–23	T̶H̶1̶	111			8
20–21	T̶H̶1̶	T̶H̶1̶	11		12
18–19	T̶H̶1̶	T̶H̶1̶	T̶H̶1̶	1	16
16–17	11				2

cy counts for age groups). A large proportion of social research is concerned with *bivariate* and *multivariate* distributions (the relation between two or more variables). If the classifications of the variables can be expressed by frequency distributions, they usually can be cross-classified and presented in tabular form. A cross-classification table is a very useful data-reduction technique, as well as a concise and vivid representation of multiple relations.

A table (which may cross-classify several variables simultaneously) is an ordered arrangement of numerical data placed in rows and columns with concise labels specifying the nature of the data. Note the clarity and ease of interpreting Table 5. Inspection of the table reveals the following patterns:

TABLE 5. *Comparison of youths who reached secondary school* (percentage distribution by birthplace and family structure)†*

TYPE OF PARENT-YOUTH RELATIONSHIP		RURAL Conjugal Pattern		URBAN Conjugal Pattern	
		Husband Makes Decisions	Both Parents Make Decisions	Husband Makes Decisions	Both Parents Make Decisions
United States	Authoritarian	34 (77)	29 (91)	50 (38)	61 (43)
	Democratic	55 (39)	59 (117)	60 (32)	76 (111)
Great Britain	Authoritarian	28 (36)	25 (69)	36 (54)	40 (75)
	Democratic	33 (24)	38 (106)	47 (62)	53 (169)
West Germany	Authoritarian	8 (73)	5 (135)	19 (83)	14 (108)
	Democratic	11 (38)	26 (68)	26 (57)	44 (106)
Italy	Authoritarian	18 (88)	26 (72)	32 (111)	29 (78)
	Democratic	47 (62)	37 (53)	58 (45)	53 (63)
Mexico	Authoritarian	5 (79)	7 (132)	13 (137)	12 (243)
	Democratic	4 (27)	14 (35)	32 (54)	39 (132)

*Adapted from Glen H. Elder, Jr., "Family Structure and Educational Attainment: A Cross-National Analysis," *American Sociological Review*, 30:91 (Table 5), February, 1965. Data from interviews of approximately 1,000 randomly selected adults eighteen and over, 1959–1960.

†The parentheses contain the total number upon which the percentages are based.

1. A greater percentage of youths in urban areas as compared with rural areas reach secondary school (by inspection of the two pairs of columns, one rural and one urban).

2. Usually the percentage of youths reaching secondary school is higher for the conjugal pattern of "both parents make decisions" than that of "husband makes decisions" (by comparing columns 1 and 3 with columns 2 and 4).

3. Democratic parent-youth relations overwhelmingly result in a higher percentage of youths reaching secondary school as compared with authoritarian relations (by inspecting rows labeled "authoritarian" and "democratic" for each of the five countries).

4. The highest percentage of youths reaching secondary school occurs in the United States, while the lowest occurs in Mexico.

5. The highest percentages usually result from a combination of democratic parent-youth relations and the conjugal pattern of "both parents make decisions."

An adequately labeled table is not difficult to read. By checking the table heading, the captions for the rows and columns, and the footnotes, a clear idea of the nature of the table is specified. This includes the nature of the sample or population, the location and the time period in which the data were collected, and who conducted the study. In analyzing the table it is often useful to check the row and the column totals, as well as the individual cell frequencies. These may reveal important patterns in the data.

In reading a table, be sure to check in which direction any percentages or rates have been computed. For example, consider Table 6. This contains four hypothetical two-by-two tables, where M stands for males, F for females, D for delinquents, and ND for nondelinquents. The first table contains the actual frequencies in a study of one hundred individuals. Cell values in A, B, and C are percentages based on the actual

TABLE 6. *Hypothetical example relating sex and delinquency by actual frequencies and percentages*

FREQUENCIES

		M	Columns	F	Total
D		20		10	30
ND	Rows	30		40	70
Total		50		50	100

PERCENTAGES

A Based on columns		B Based on rows		C Based on the total	
M	F	M	F	M	F
D 40	20	D 67	33	D 20	10
ND 60	80	ND 43	57	ND 30	40

Key: M Males
     F Females
     D Delinquents
     ND Nondelinquents

frequency cross-tabulations. *A* has percentages based on the column total, *B* on the row total, and *C* on the total number in the whole table (100). The three percentage distributions are significantly different from each other, and each cell must be carefully interpreted. For example, consider the 40 percent (20 is 40 percent of 50) in *A* for the cell crossing *M* and *D* (i.e., the first cell). This is interpreted to mean that 40 percent of the males in the sample are delinquent. It is wrong to interpret this 40 percent as delinquents in the sample who are male (67 percent, as shown in *B*) or as the percentage of male delinquents in the total sample (20 percent, as shown in *C*). The 57 percent in *B* represents the percentage of nondelinquents in the sample who are female. How would you interpret the 20 percent in *A,* the 43 percent in *B,* and the 10 percent in *C?* If you were interested in determining whether or not sex causes delinquency, which percentage table would be most appropriate?

TYPICAL VALUES   The average score or class of a variable often is referred to as the typical value or central tendency. The average is an important measure because it reduces the data to one highly meaningful value that is readily grasped and easily communicated. An average value simplifies a wide range of experiences and is one way of making sense out of the empirical world. We often hear statements about and think in terms of the average man, the average weight for a given height, the typical baby, the modal response, and the common way of doing something.

The three averages most commonly used in social research are the *mode,* the *median,* and the arithmetic *mean.* Consider the frequency distribution shown in Table 7.

The mode is simply the category (or categories) containing the highest frequency; in this instance, it is the category designating three close friends in college ($f = 6$). If two categories had six individuals each, the distribution would be *bimodal.*

The median is the category or point above and below which 50 percent of the total frequency lies, or it is the middle category dividing the distribution into two equal parts. In the example of close friends in college, the median is the category

TABLE 7.   *Hypothetical example of typical values based on college friendships*

NUMBER OF CLOSE FRIENDS IN COLLEGE (X)	FREQUENCY (f)	FREQUENCY OF CONTACT WITH CLOSE FRIENDS (fX)
4	2	8
3	6	18
2	5	10
1	4	4
0	4	0
	21*	40

*The sum of the frequencies is 21, or $\Sigma f = N = 21$.

designating two close friends, because above and below that category are eight cases, respectively.

The mean is the arithmetic average, which is the sum of all the scores divided by their number:

$$\overline{X} = \frac{\Sigma f X}{N}$$

The statistical symbol for the mean is $\overline{X}$; $\Sigma f X$ means to add up all the scores, and N is the number of scores (or individuals). In the example of the close friends in college, we must consider the fact that each friendship category has more than one individual; e.g., two individuals have four close friends, and six have three close friends. To compute the $\Sigma f X$, we add 4 twice, 3 six times, 2 five times, 1 four times, and 0 four times. This can easily be computed by constructing the $\Sigma f X$ column and summing the scores to a total of 40. Since N is 21 (the number of individuals), the mean ($\overline{X}$) is 40/21 or 1.9. The mean can be conceived of as a fulcrum point, so that the weights of the scores above and below the mean are equal and therefore balanced.

The three averages have different advantages and limitations. The mean has two major advantages over the median and the mode. First, the mean has a wider statistical application and can be manipulated in more ways. For example, it is tied to several other statistics that may be important for analysis. Second, the mean is more stable in a sampling sense than are the other two averages. In other words, the means from two random samples of the same population are more likely to be closer in value than the corresponding medians or modes. Often counteracting these advantages, however, are two limitations. First, the mean is limited in applicability to quantitative variables (measured by numbers). It is not used for getting typical values of qualitative or rank-order data. Second, the mean may be unduly affected by one or a few extreme scores. To illustrate, if everyone but one in a population of one thousand made $8,000 a year and the one "deviant" made 6 million, the mean income for that population would be $13,992 (a highly misleading average). Consequently, the median, which is not affected by extreme scores, is the best average for such distributions. Furthermore, the median may be used on numbered and rank-order variables.

The mode has the advantages of being easy and quick to compute and is the only average that can be interpreted for qualitative data. It is, however, a highly unstable average because if categories are grouped or if one more individual is added its value can be altered substantially.

DISPERSION   The differences among the scores of a distribution (e.g., differences among college students with regard to the grade-point average) are commonly referred to as dispersion, variation, spread, or scatter. While the average yields the typical score in a distribution, a measure of dispersion indicates the amount of spread or difference among the scores. To combat such notions that a "statistician cannot drown in a lake averaging three feet in depth," or that a "statistician with his head in the oven and feet in the refrigerator is OK because on the average he is normal," a dispersion measure should, whenever possible, be computed along with the average. There is an obvious difference between two individuals who have an averaged score of 90 on three exams, given the following: individual *A* scored 80, 90, and 100; individual *B* scored 88, 90, and 92. Although they average the same, a dispersion measure indicates the greater consistency of *B,* and the somewhat sporadic performance of *A*.

There are two basic ways of measuring dispersion: measures based on a range of scores and those based on deviations from an average score (the mean or the median).

Measurements of *range* are based either on the total spread of scores (that is, the highest minus the lowest scores) or on the difference between two intermediate values. For example, two commonly used measures based on intermediate values are (1) the *10th–90th percentile range,* which encompasses the middle 80 percent of the scores in a distribution, and (2) the *interquartile range,* that is, the first to fourth quartiles or the 25th–75th percentile range, which encompasses the middle 50 percent. Because one extreme score can make the total range excessively large and misleading, ranges based on the intermediate values rather than on the total range generally prove more useful for descriptive purposes. Given the distribution of ages in Table 4, the total range is 9 (25–16);[1] the 10th–90th percentile range is 5.46; and the interquartile range is 3.l6. The total range of 9 means that all scores lie within 9 years; the 10th–90th range means that the middle 80 percent of individuals lie within 5.46 years; and finally, the interquartile range indicates that the middle 50 percent of the individuals lie within 3.16 years.

The range measures reflect only two scores in the total distribution—that is, the 90th and 10th percentiles, or the 75th and 25th percentiles. They do not reflect the variation of each particular score; consequently, they ignore many scores in a distribution. Dispersion measures based on deviations from an average (average deviation and standard deviation) reflect each score in the distribution and usually yield more useful and stable measures than those based on range.

Based on deviations from an average, the *average deviation* considers each score's difference from the mean or median. Differences between the individual's score (X) and the average score ($\bar{X}$) are summed, taking the absolute value (that is, the differences are considered positive and are added together). The resulting sum of the deviation scores is divided by the number of individuals (N), which yields the mean deviation score.

$$AD_{\bar{x}} = \frac{\Sigma |X - \bar{X}|}{N}$$

The symbol Σ stands for summing all values. For the distribution in Table 7, the average deviation from the mean (AD) is 1.07. To

[1]Figured on the basis of the true upper and lower limits, the range is 10 (25.5–15.5).

interpret, the individual scores vary from the mean score by an average of 1.07 units—that is, 1.07 close friends in college.

The *standard deviation* is based on the squared deviations from the mean of the distribution. The differences between each X score and the $\overline{X}$ is squared and summed, divided by N to obtain an average value, and finally the square root is taken of this value:

$$s = \sqrt{\frac{\Sigma(X - \overline{X})^2}{N}}$$

The square of the standard deviation(s) is called the variance (s^2) and is an important dispersion measure in its own right in classical statistics. The standard deviation is usually interpreted in either of two ways: (1) as a relative index number, roughly indicating which of two or more distributions is more dispersed (for example, the dispersion on age in Table 4 [$s = 2.02$] is greater than the dispersion on number of close friends in Table 7 [$s = 1.27$], and (2) when applied to a population distributed in a particular way (normally distributed), s indicates the percentage of individuals that lie between any two scores in the distribution. That is, in a normal distribution, roughly 34 percent of the cases lie between the $\overline{X}$ and one standard deviation. If the age distribution in Table 4 were normal, the s of 2.02 would mean that 34 percent of the cases lie roughly between the ages of twenty and twenty-two. As another example, assuming that IQ scores are normally distributed with a mean of 100 and an s of 10, then about 68 percent of all cases have scores between 90 and 110 (which is about one normal standard-deviation unit above and below the mean).

The standard deviation has two definite advantages over the average deviation. It is related to a large number of other statistical techniques and is more readily manipulated; for example, standard deviations of two different samples can be combined. The average deviation is not, however, as highly influenced by extreme scores in a distribution. Consequently, one or a few extreme scores can inflate the value of the standard deviation and render it nearly useless as an indicator of spread. The average deviation is preferable in such cases.

RELATIONS   The association between two variables results from a cross-tabulation of scores in two distributions and can be presented either in tabular form (as in Table 6) or it can be graphed or charted pictorially. For example, consider Table 8, which represents the cross-tabulated relation between education and the number of community organizations of which respondents are members (by frequency tallies in the cells).

The cross-tabulation in Table 8 shows a definite positive relation between the number of years of formal education and the number of community organizations in which an individual holds membership. To some extent, the higher the educational level, the larger is the number of memberships held in community organizations. Note that the relation is not perfect. For example, the fourteen persons with twelve to fourteen years of education range all the way from one to seven organizational

TABLE 8.   *Hypothetical cross-tabulation of years of formal education with individual membership in community organizations*

YEARS OF FORMAL EDUCATION	NUMBER OF COMMUNITY ORGANIZATIONS							
	0	1	2	3	4	5	6	7
18–20						1	11	1111
15–17			1	111	11	11	11	
12–14		1	111	11	11	111	11	1
9–11	11	111	11	1	1	1		
6–8	1	1	1	1				
3–5	111	1	1					
0–2	11	1	1					

memberships, although the average number of organizations is higher than that for the nine- to eleven-year educational category and lower than the fifteen- to seventeen-year category. In short, there is a direct, but far from perfect, relation between the two variables. The problem is to reduce this relation to one summary measure (value) that adequately describes the degree to which the two variables vary together.

Other examples of associations, or "the way things go together," are facial expressions and anger, intelligence and grades, criminal acts and punishment, seasons and riots, rain and crop yield, and anomie and suicide. In science such relations are established on a rigorous and interpretable basis by the use of statistical techniques that indicate the degree to which two or more variables are related.

Relationship measures are based on two underlying principles—the principle of *covariation* and the principle of *joint occurrence.*

Covariation refers to relations between variables quantitatively measured and applies to the case where a unit change in one variable is paralleled with some degree of regularity by a comparable change in another variable. That is, two variables somehow move together. If two variables are directly related, then increases (or decreases) in one variable are paralleled by increases (or decreases) in the other. An inverse relation based on the principle of covariation occurs when an increase in one variable is paralleled by a decrease in the other variable. For example, Elder found an inverse relation between parental dominance and scholastic progress—that is, the more dominant the parent, the less the child's progress.

Two frequently used measures based on this principle are the correlation coefficient (r) for quantitative variables and Spearman's rho (ρ) for rank-order variables. Both measures yield a value between -1 and $+1$, where 0 indicates no relation between two variables and the two extremes indicate a perfect negative relation (-1) and a perfect direct relation ($+1$). The degree of relation based on these two measures indicates the degree to which two variables covary. With regard to the data in Table 8, r is .75 and ρ is .93.

The most common interpretation of the correlation coefficient (r) is in terms of r^2 as variance explained. Variance is a measure of the amount of differences in scores or values among individuals. The square of the correlation coefficient indicates the proportion of the variance in one variable (in the example in Table 8, memberships in community organizations) that is explained by (accounted for, or attributable to) the variance in another variable (in the example, years of formal education). Therefore, about 56 percent ($.75^2$) of the variance in organizational membership is accounted for by variance in formal education. Compared with many relations found in the social sciences, this is a rather high correlation, although approximately 46 percent of the variance is not accounted for by education. At this point in social analysis, the researcher should usually look for other predictor variables to explain even more of the variance in memberships.

Spearman's rho is a measure of relation usually applied to rank-order data and refers to the degree of agreement between two rank orders. Consider the following example in Table 9. The rho value between class and friendship choice is $-.88$, which indicates a high inverse relation between the two rank orders. According to these hypothetical data, the higher the social class, the fewer the friendship choices. Rho is a fairly simple measure to compute by hand, and for many bivariate distributions it is an adequate summary measure of the relation.

Measures of association based on the principle of joint occurrence are most often applied to qualitative variables. Joint occurrence refers to the idea that any unit, such as an individual, can be placed in several categories simultaneously. For example, an individual may be a rich male, a poor Catholic, a highly educated criminal, a brilliant writer, or a witty student. The relation is established by discovering if one category is frequently occupied by another category; for example, sex and occupation. There are many measures based on joint occurrence. Two rather simple ones are *lambda* and Yule's *Q*. Consider the hypothetical data in Table 10, which cross-tabulates marital happiness by sex.

Lambda yields a clear interpretation of this cross-

TABLE 9   *Hypothetical example of relating the rank order of social class to the rank order of friendship*

INDI-VIDUAL	SOCIAL CLASS (X)	NUMBER OF TIMES CHOSEN AS A CLOSE FRIEND (Y)	RANK OF X	RANK OF Y	DIF-FERENCE (d)	d^2
Bob	Upper-upper	0	1	7	6	36
Hal	Lower-upper	2	2	6	4	16
Erika	Upper-middle	3	3	5	2	4
Ricky	Lower-middle	4	4.5	3.5	1	1
Karen	Lower-middle	5	4.5	2	2.5	6.25
Jerry	Upper-lower	4	6	3.5	2.5	6.25
Sandy	Lower-lower	6	7	1	6	36

$$\rho = 1 - \frac{6\Sigma d^2}{N(N^2 - 1)} \qquad N = 7 \qquad \Sigma d^2 = 105.5$$

$$\rho = 1 - \frac{6(105.5)}{7(7^2 - 1)}$$

$$\rho = 1 - \frac{630}{336}$$

$$\rho = 1 - 1.875$$

$$\rho = -.875$$

$$\rho = -.88$$

classification. Without detailing the procedure, lambda is .25, which represents a 25 percent reduction in error over guessing about marital happiness without knowing the sex of the individual. Specifically, this measure indicates the proportionate reduction in error by using a predictor variable over the original error, which is based on choosing the largest marginal frequency in the dependent variable. Stated otherwise, reduction in error is measured by the proportion of erroneous predictions, without knowing the sex of the subject, of who will be happily married to the erroneous predictions with such knowledge. If we had only the one choice that persons were either happily married or not

TABLE 10. *Hypothetical example relating sex to marital happiness*

	MALES	FEMALES
Happily married	30	10
Not happily married	20	40

happily married, we would predict the latter and be wrong forty times (because forty are happily married and sixty are not). With knowledge of the person's sex, we would predict that males are happily married and we would be wrong twenty times; and we would predict that females are not happily married and we would be wrong ten times. We have reduced our original prediction error by ten (forty errors without knowledge of sex and thirty with such knowledge), and ten out of forty is a 25 percent reduction in error.

In contrast to lambda, which can be used in any table (no matter how many rows and columns), Yule's Q is strictly for the two-by-two table. Yule's Q is defined as:

$$Q = \frac{ad - bc}{ad + bc}$$

The first cell (first row, first column) is referred to in the equation by a, b refers to the second cell (first row, second column), c refers to the third cell (second row, first column), and d refers to the fourth cell (second row, second column). Schematically, the notations are given as follows:

a	b
c	d

Q can be interpreted in two ways: (1) as a departure from a state of independence and (2) in terms of error reduction. The first interpretation is based on the idea that if two variables are independent, they are not related. In the hypothetical example, if males and females are equally likely to be happily or unhappily married, then sex and marital happiness are independent. In the example, this is obviously not the case. Substituting the values in Table 10 into the equation for Q yields a measure of .71, which indicates a substantial departure from independence. The second interpretation of Q, based on error reduction, is more complex than the lambda interpretation. However, it also involves an original error prediction without using the independent variable (sex), and then a new prediction error using the variable. The .71 value for Q represents a 71 percent error reduction. Q and lambda have different values because they are based on different error predictions.

There are many relationship measures, and each one may be interpreted in ways different from the others. Consequently, for specific interpretations, the nature of each measure must be specified. Some measures are easy to interpret, while others are unclear in their meanings. Measures often used in sociology are *r, eta, gamma, tau, rho, lambda, C* (coefficient of contingency), *dyx,* and *phi.* For exact interpretations or for problems in interpretations, the reader should consult statistical textbooks. In general, however, these measures indicate relations of covariation (two or more variables moving together) or joint occurrence (simultaneous placement of individuals into two or more categories). Measures of relations, for the most part, are standardized to have values between 0 and 1 or -1 and $+1$. Values close to 0 indicate a low relation, while those near 1 or -1 indicate a high relation.

MULTIVARIATE TECHNIQUES   Scientific study often interrelates three or more variables. The basic reasons for studying more than just one dependent and one independent variable are *control* and *prediction.* Any particular problem may call for holding the effects of a variable constant (control), or it may call for utilization of independent (causal) variables to explain or account for variation in a dependent variable (prediction). In other words, these techniques are used to either predict the values of one variable by the values of several variables, or to find out the relation between two variables if the effects of other variables are taken out.

Since most social scientists think that phenomena have multiple causes, multivariate techniques are often used to relate three or more variables. The most prominent technique is the prediction of a dependent variable (for example, number of organizational memberships) by an additive combination of two or more independent variables (for example, education and occupational prestige). The counterpart to the bivariate correlation coefficient (r) is the multiple R, which is based upon one dependent variable and two or more independent variables. Multiple R also may be interpreted as variance explained—that is, the amount of variance in the dependent variable that is accounted for by an additive combination of the variation in the independent variables. Education or occupational prestige alone may account for no more than 25 percent of the variance in organizational memberships, but in an additive combination, they may account for 50 percent.

Three widely used controlling procedures are *subclassification, norming,* and *standardization.* Control of a variable means to take out (almost always only in part) the effects of a factor, and thus make visible a more nearly "pure" relation between the variables under consideration. As an illustration of control by subclassification (or partialling), consider the association between storks and babies (which, depending on time and place, is almost always small but positive). Few people believe that storks bring babies, and the small positive relation is undoubtedly due to rural areas having both a larger number of storks and a higher birth rate than urban areas. To take out the effects of urbanization, the relation between storks and babies is computed separately for urban and rural areas. To illustrate, consider the three two-by-two cross-tabulations in Table 11. Cross-tabulation A shows a strong relation between storks and babies when urban and rural areas are considered together; but by cross-tabulating the data separately for urban areas (B) and rural areas (C), the relation no longer exists. Urbanization is controlled by being held rather crudely constant with regard to

TABLE 11. *Hypothetical example of controlling for a third variable*

	A ALL AREAS			B URBAN AREAS			C RURAL AREAS	
	Number of storks	*Number of babies*		*Number of storks*	*Number of babies*		*Number of storks*	*Number of babies*
	High	Low		High	Low		High	Low
High	10	0	High	0	0	High	10	0
Low	0	10	Low	0	10	Low	0	0

the variables in question. More adequate control, of course, would consider many more gradations of urbanization besides the rather gross dichotomy of rural-urban.

Norming controls for a third factor by including it in the actual values of a variable. Examples of norming are percentages, proportions, ratios, and indexes. To illustrate, for most problems there is little sense in comparing the states of New York and Nevada on the total number of births, deaths, suicides, crimes, business establishments, or labor unions. Obviously, New York is far ahead of Nevada on all of these because of its large number of people. Even if New York had a low birth rate and Nevada had a high one, New York would show a much greater number of births. If we want to compare these two states meaningfully on such variables, we must take out or control for the overwhelming factor of differential size.

It can be done simply by computing percentages or rates. Instead of computing births, deaths, suicides, and crimes, we compute birth rates, death rates, suicide rates, and crime rates. A rate controls for population size by making it a constant. For example, the suicide rate is the number of people committing suicide in a given year divided by the mid-year population and multiplied by 100,000. Any population, large or small, will have a rate expressed in terms of a standard 100,000. By eliminating population size as a dominant factor, meaningful comparisons can be made. Percentages provide the same kind of control. To say that fifty people in group *A* and one hundred in group *B* had fewer cavities is not a meaningful comparison until we know the size of the groups. If there were one hundred people in group *A* and four hundred in group *B,* then 50 percent of *A* and only 25 percent of *B* had fewer cavities.

Standardization provides a single summary measure of an observed distribution by adjusting the data to one or more characteristics of a constant (i.e., standard) distribution. For example, Florida has a higher death rate than New York. The higher rate may be due to the larger percentage of older people in Florida. Note that control by norming has already been accomplished by basing the comparison on rates. It may be important, however, to know what the death rates would be if the two populations had the same age distribution (in this instance, an equal percentage in each age group). This can be accomplished by standardizing both states on the age distribution of the United States, thereby controlling for the effects of age on the death rates. If Florida still has a higher rate, then it is not due to the age factor.

In other words, we answer the question, "If New York and Florida had the same proportion of people in each age category, what would be their respective death rates?" There are a variety of techniques to adjust the data to answer this question. One frequently used method is first to compute the age-specific death rates for the existing populations, and then to apply these death rates to the adjusted number of people in the age groups in the standard population. The standard population may be a hypothetical model, where there are an equal number of people in all age groups, or it may be a real model, such as the age distribution for the United States in 1975. The major advantage of standardization is that it provides a single summary measure for comparative purposes.

inference

Given knowledge of a sample, the problem of inference is to say something about a population. If 10 percent of a sample of youths are delinquent, what can we say about the percentage of delinquents in the population?

Statistical inference is based on probability statements, which ultimately leads to a decision based on the budgeting of an error rate. That is, there is always an element of error in any conclusion based on inference statistics. Based on probability, however, we can state what that risk or error is when trying to choose between, say, two hypotheses.

Consider, for example, a panel of experts who claim that they can predict which of any two countries will have a greater number of riots in a given period. Suppose that we pair off a number of countries and ask the panel to make their predictions. Suppose also that they successfully select the more riot-torn countries in the first two pairs. Are we willing to say at this point that the panel has the knowledge to differentiate countries as to frequency of riots? It is not likely that they would guess correctly twice in a row, but this likelihood is too high for us to conclude that their predictions are based on knowledge. This is comparable to using an unbiased coin, where the outcome (heads or tails) of the first two tosses will be guessed correctly 25 percent of the time. The chance of guessing correctly twice in a row the countries that will have outbreaks of riots is so high (25 percent) that we would want more proof that the panel truly had the knowledge to predict frequency of riots.

Suppose, now, that the panel of experts correctly differentiates the first five pairs of countries. Would we now be willing to say that the panel can predict those countries that will have riots? Comparing this case with the unbiased coin, correctly guessing the outcome of the first five tosses, on the basis of chance alone, occurs only about 3 percent of the time. At this point we may conclude that the panel truly has this predictive ability, because there is small chance (only three times in one hundred) that by guessing they correctly distinguished between the first five pairs of countries.

If this is still too great a risk, we could give the panel more pairs of countries. At some point, however, we make a decision as to whether they do or do not have the knowledge to predict. Since we cannot or do not test all cases, there is always some risk that we are wrong in our conclusions. For example, it is not likely that a person will make seventeen passes in a row at the dice table, but it does happen. If we accuse him of using "loaded" dice, we may well be wrong. If, however, someone did make seventeen passes in a row, we would bet on him to make the eighteenth, because there are only two ways of making seventeen passes in a row—either the player is extremely lucky or he is crooked.

To illustrate the nature of inference, consider the following hypothetical test. Suppose at a college or university we polled a sample of undergraduate students with regard to their attitudes toward premarital intercourse. Let us set up the hypothesis that, since college students sometimes break away from the general norms of society, most students will favor premarital intercourse (at least between engaged couples). Now, out of a sample of 120 students, 70 favor premarital intercourse and 50 are opposed on any grounds. If we concluded at this point that the hypothesis was supported, we would be neglecting possible sampling error. It may be that these 120 students do not adequately represent the total student body. We are not interested in the sample per se, but in the population it represents.

If all students had been polled and approximately 58 percent (70 is about 58 percent of 120) favored premarital intercourse, then the hypothesis is supported. There can be no sampling error if the total population is polled. Furthermore, the larger the sample, the more likely it is that the sample is representative. Small samples, on the other hand, may be in error (that is, do not represent the population) to a rather large degree. Consequently, sample size determines (partially) the degree of risk taken in inferring the results of the sample to the population (the larger the sample, the less the risk). Another important determinant of the degree of risk taken in inference is the amount of dispersion (differences) in the population. If all else is equal, the greater the differences, the greater the risk taken.

With regard to the example, the problem is to determine whether or not a 58/42 percent split in the sample could have reasonably occurred by chance from a population that is actually characterized by a 50/50 split. If there is an even split in the population, then 60 out of 120 students would favor premarital intercourse, barring sampling error. If the 50/50 split truly represents the population, then the 58/42 percent split (70/50 numerical split) in the sample can only be due to sampling errors. The task of testing the hypothesis is to provide a basis for making a reasonable choice between the two alternatives: (1) Is the split indicated by the sample merely a chance deviation from the even split in the population, or (2) is the population not evenly split?

Without going into the details of hypothesis testing, whether or not a 58/42 percent (70/50) split in the sample could have reasonably come from a population that actually has a 50/50 percent split is dependent partially on sample size. To test this, we need to determine how likely it is to get a 70/50 split from a sample of 120 persons when a 60/60 split is predicted. If it is not likely, then we would reject the hypothesis of a 50/50 population split and conclude that most of the college students favor premarital intercourse.

To determine the deviation of 70 (actual) minus 60 (predicted), we need an estimate of the sampling error. The sampling error is based on the same principle as the standard deviation. While the standard deviation refers to the spread or dispersion of scores in a distribution, the sampling error refers to the spread or dispersion of sample characteristics. In this example, a large number of samples of 120 students may show responses favoring premarital intercourse that vary from less than 50 to over 100.

An estimate of the sampling error is determined by the equation $s_p = \sqrt{Npq}$, where s_p is the sampling error of a proportion: p is the probability of favoring premarital intercourse. The actual (70) minus the predicted (60), which is 10, divided by s_p provides the necessary estimate of sampling error. In this case, s_p is 5.45, $\sqrt{120(\frac{1}{2})(\frac{1}{2})}$. When 5.45 is divided into 10, we get 1.84. Now this 1.84 could have occurred by chance from an evenly split population about three times in 100. Since it could occur by chance so infrequently, we are likely to reject the hypothesis that the total student population of the college is evenly split on attitudes toward premarital intercourse, and would conclude that most students favor it.

One commonly used test of hypotheses in sociology is a statistic called *chi square* (x^2). The x^2 test indicates the probability of the observed cross-tabulated distribution of two attributes or variables resulting from purely chance factors. For example, consider the data in Table 10, which is a cross-tabulation of sex by marital happiness. For the above table, $x^2 = 16.67$. A value of this size for a two-by-two table indicates that the relation between sex and marital happiness (that is, males are predominantly happy while females are not) is probably not a chance occurrence. Actually, from a population where there is no relation between the two attributes, this relation could have occurred by chance less than one time in a thousand (this is usually reported as $p < .001$). Consequently, we conclude there is a non-zero relation between sex and marital happiness.

In the social sciences, if a relation could occur by chance less than five times or one time in one hundred ($p < .05$ or $p < .01$), it is generally considered statistically significant. That is, it can reasonably be assumed that the sample relation did not come from a population characterized by a relation of zero. There are several measures of statistical significance: e.g., critical ratio, F ratio, t-test, chi-square, Mann-Whitney U, the median test, the sign test, and the runs test. Each of these tests gives an indication of the reasonableness of inferring from the sample to the population. They are applied to different problems, depending upon the level of measurement, sample size, and the number of variables in question.

summary

Statistical techniques are used to reduce a large amount of data to a few meaningful measures that can be reasonably handled and compared. Statistics can be divided into description and inference. Descriptive statistics are computed to determine the characteristics of the data at hand, while inference statistics are used to estimate the characteristics of the population from which the sample was drawn.

Under descriptive statistics, univariate, bivariate, and multivariate techniques were presented. Two univariate techniques of primary importance are typical values (averages) and dispersion or spread (such as range measures and the standard deviation). These are based on frequency distributions, which often is the necessary first step in data analysis. The correlation coefficient r, Spearman's rho, Yule's Q, and lambda were given as bivariate relation measures. Relation measures are basically of two types—those based on covariation (r and rho) and those based on joint occurrence (Q and lambda). Multivariate techniques are used to interrelate three or more variables, usually for control or prediction purposes. The three controlling procedures of subclassification, norming, and standardization were discussed.

Techniques of inference permit researchers, given knowledge of a sample, to make statements about a population. Statistical inference is based on probability statements and always involves an element of risk. In other words, these techniques tell us the risk we are taking owing to the sample not being representative of the population, so that reasonable decisions can be made.

references

Anderson, Theodore R., and Morris Zelditch, Jr. 1975. *A Basic Course in Statistics.* 3rd ed. New York: Holt, Rinehart & Winston, Inc.

Blalock, Hubert M. 1970. *Social Statistics.* 2nd ed. New York: McGraw-Hill Book Company.

Mueller, John H., Karl F. Schuessler, and Herbert Costner. 1970. *Statistical Reasoning in Sociology.* 2nd ed. Boston: Houghton Mifflin Company.

Chapter 7

Decision Making in Scientific Research

The scientific method can be treated as a series of decision-making steps. The researcher must decide, among other things, on the focus of his problem, the variables, measurement procedures, design, and sampling techniques. The burden is on the researcher to select the most advantageous alternatives. Consequently, before conducting the research, the selected problem should be thoroughly thought out, and relevant literature should be read. That is, the researcher should begin his study with as much knowledge about his subject matter as possible. He should then carefully think through each step. He may not be able, in all cases, to follow his original plan, but he is less likely to be surprised and the study is more likely to be reliable and important if such a plan exists.

The purpose of this chapter is to illustrate several points made earlier by leading the reader through a series of decision-making steps in carrying out social research. We have selected the problem of student evaluations of teaching as our example, so the remaining decisions to be made are: (1) conceptual framework, (2) population and sample, (3) research design, (4) methods of observation, and (5) data analysis. Although the actual study is not carried out, relevant decisions are indicated in each of these five areas.

conceptual framework

The research problem is to determine some consequences of the effect of student evaluations of teachers' performances. Under the conceptual framework, it is the researcher's task to specify clearly the major concepts and variables, the testable hypotheses, and the rationales or theories justifying the hypotheses. Consider the following three related hypotheses and their rationales.

HYPOTHESIS 1   The first hypothesis stipulates that, as student evaluations are increasingly considered by administrators as a major criterion for teacher rewards (promotions and salary raises), the teacher will lower his grading standards in the classroom. The rationale in support of this hypothesis is the following: Teachers will become more lenient in grading because this will increase their popularity with students. Further, the more popular teachers will receive the most favorable evaluations. This rationale is based on the assumption that persons select the means that most readily lead to the rewards of the situation. In this instance, lowering the grading standards seems to be a direct line to a favorable evaluation. It should be noted that one or more aspects of the rationale may be false; for example, some students (perhaps those with high grade-point averages) may negatively evaluate lenient graders. Consequently, if the hypothesis is supported by the research, this is interpreted only as being *consistent* with the rationale. It does not prove the rationale to be true, even though it does support it. Actually, many supportive studies are required before confidence can be placed in the rationale (and the hypothesis).

HYPOTHESIS 2   The second hypothesis maintains that the more that administrators emphasize student evaluations as a major criterion for teacher promotions and salary raises, the lower will be teacher morale and the higher will be student morale. The supporting rationale for this hypothesis primarily is based on the notion that those who take a meaningful part in the decision-making process are not only more involved in the situation, but will feel more important. Consequently, their morale will rise. Teachers, however, must now please students as well as the administration, which means that there are more persons with power over them. It is also likely that students increase their power position at the expense of the power of the teacher. These factors should lower teacher morale.

HYPOTHESIS 3   According to the third hypothesis, the greater the discrepancy between the ideal and real criteria for evaluating teacher performance, the less time teachers will spend in the teacher "role." That is, if the effectiveness of teaching course material is supposed to be evaluated (ideal) by administrators, but teachers are evaluated as entertainers, nice guys, sharp dressers, or sympathetic listeners (actual), teachers will spend less time on course material and on preparing lectures, will assign fewer exams and papers, and will have a higher absentee rate.

If administrators use student evaluations of teachers to assess teaching effectiveness, there will be a strong likelihood of a substantial discrepancy between the ideal and real in teacher evaluations. Stated otherwise, administrators accept student non-ideal evaluations as if they were based on the ideal. Because there is no agreed-upon, observable way of evaluating good teaching, it is probable that other more-measurable characteristics will be selected for evaluation. It is assumed that persons select measurables for evaluation because these are more understandable and justifiable. Further, it is difficult for a student to evaluate the effectiveness of teaching when he is largely ignorant of the subject matter and the problems in the area. Also, it is sometimes difficult to know whether you have learned something, let alone to know how correct or relevant to the field is the knowledge. More measurable characteristics to the student appear to be the teacher's mannerisms, style of dress, entertaining qualities, and friendliness.

CONCEPTS   There are nine basic concepts associated with the three hypotheses and related rationales. These are: student evaluations, morale, classroom standards, rewards (promotions and salary increases), measurable characteristics, popularity, ideal evaluational criteria, real evaluational criteria, and the teacher role. Six of these concepts must be operationalized (made observable) to permit empirical tests of the three hypotheses: student evaluations, classroom standards, morale (for both students and teachers), ideal evaluational criteria, real evaluational criteria, and the teacher role. Their operational definitions are treated in the section on observational techniques.

population and sample

It is necessary to decide first on the nature and size of the population and then on the type and size of the sample. These decisions not only are tied closely to the research problem and conceptual framework, but they should also be based on the research design, observational techniques, and methods selected for data analysis. Consequently, although the scientific method is treated as a distinct set of decisions, in actual practice most decisions are made with simultaneous consideration of the various steps. Moreover, several additional factors may be influencing decisions; such factors range from the time, money, and effort available for the research to available research facilities, the competence of research assistance, and the moral implications of the problem.

DECISIONS ON THE NATURE AND SIZE OF THE POPULATION

One of the first decisions to be made concerns the inclusiveness of the population. A study encompassing all teachers and students in all grade levels everywhere seems well beyond the capabilities of any one or several investigators (given present research technology). Therefore, a decision must be made to delimit the population to a manageable size. The three most prominent factors determining the scope of the population are (1) the number of different grades and school levels, (2) the number and size of geographical areas, and (3) the number of time periods studied. The decision about grade or school level must consider the fact that schools include colleges, universities, high schools, junior high schools, grade schools, and various professional and technical schools. Since student evaluations are more prevalent and have a greater effect in colleges or universities, we may decide to exclude all other grades or schools. Moreover, in regard to geographic areas, we may decide to select only "developed" countries in the Western world (or just the United States) because these countries have educational systems that are drastically different from those in "underdeveloped" countries in the East. Once a decision has been made to select one or more countries, a similar line of reasoning is used to select divisions within a country—that is, regions, states, provinces, counties, etc. Funds may limit us to colleges and universities in the United States or, perhaps, to one state or even to one college. Finally, a decision must be made on whether to delimit the study to one point in time or to several. The study of several colleges over time may be crucial to testing the hypothesis that student evaluations and low class standards are interrelated. The hypothesis may be true, but class standards may decline only after a few years elapse from the start of student evaluations.

DECISIONS ON THE TYPE AND SIZE OF THE SAMPLE   Let us suppose that the population is limited to undergraduate students at colleges and universities in the United States. Given the large student body this represents, a sample is required. Decisions on the sample must consider the types of colleges and universities, the areas of the United States, the size of the sample of colleges and universities, and the size of the sample of students and professors in any particular college or university. For example, we may want to limit the inquiry to public schools, or just to state colleges, or to schools in the Eastern states, or perhaps to colleges with a student enrollment of over fifteen thousand. Separate decisions may be necessary for each college or university selected. Should you select all students in all courses or just a sample of students and courses? If students (and courses or professors) are to be sampled, how many should be selected, and should the sample be stratified on such characteristics as the student's major (social sciences, physical sciences, humanities, etc.), class standing (freshman, sophomore, junior, and senior), or socioeconomic status? This by no means exhausts all the possibilities, but merely illustrates the complexity of the decision-making process. Depending on the resources, an adequate inquiry may be made only on one or a few colleges. If so, a judicious (nonrandom) selection of colleges may be made. This choice can be made on the most "typical" college in an area. For example, the typical college should be coeducational, around twenty thousand students, and located in an urban area. Once the few colleges are selected, random sampling may be applied to each one.

research design

The nature of the problem and how the problem is conceptualized are major factors in the selection of a research design. To illustrate, if the problem is in a relatively unexplored area (where little is known), an intensive case study may be the most appropriate choice. A thorough scrutiny of one or a few classrooms or schools may suggest important propositions about student evaluations. Furthermore, if the researcher decides that experiencing student and teacher reactions and motives is crucial to the inquiry, he may have to observe them closely in the classroom situation over an extended period of time. If, however, something is known about the subject matter and the researcher feels that his own conceptualization of the problem is important, he may decide on utilizing a social survey or an experimental design.

Regardless of the design selected, observations must be made with regard to each of the major concepts. Alternative techniques for these observations are discussed in the following section. A survey requires observations of either a sample or a population—in this case, of opinions, attitudes, and behavior patterns of students and teachers in selected schools. If a single point in time is selected for study, it may be good research strategy to select schools that vary on the independent variables. For example, one or more of the schools should be high in the effectiveness of student evaluations and should show wide discrepancy between ideal and real evaluational criteria; others in the design should be low in effectiveness and should show small discrepancies. This type of design may be designated as *correlational* or *synchronic*.

In this study it may be best to survey, by means of a panel or a poll, the sample of persons at two points in time, rather than at just one time. A poll is the study of two different samples over a period of time, while a panel is the repeated study of one sample. A panel or poll design increases the expense and effort, but a time differential may be necessary to allow the independent variables to take effect. The panel appears to be the most adequate design for the problem we are considering because (1) it permits the study of the change process through an analysis of change scores, and (2) it is conducive to isolating the time priority of variables (see Chapter 4).

In the panel design, cross-lagged relations that are based on time priorities may be evaluated. For example, with regard to Hypothesis 2, there may be a considerable lag in time after student evaluations are formally introduced as a major criterion for teacher promotions and salary raises until teacher morale decreases (or student morale increases). The morale of teachers (or students) may not be immediately affected, because they either may not believe that student evaluations will be effective or they are unaware of the consequences of such evaluations. Presumably after a certain lag in time, teachers (and students) will realize the importance of the evaluations and react accordingly. The panel design permits an assessment of this potential time lag. By studying the same group at two points in time, we can check schools that used student evaluations as a major criterion in the first observation period and then check the morale level of both groups (student and teacher) at the second observation period.

To illustrate a test by an experimental technique, consider Hypothesis 1, which states that as student evaluations are increasingly considered by administrators as a major criterion for teacher rewards, the teacher will lower his grading standards in the classroom. Suppose a series of small-group experiments is devised in which the subjects are comprised of five students and one teacher. The teacher will grade the subjects on their performance in completing a task (such as solving a puzzle). The subjects should be as comparable as possible from one experiment to the next (that is, they should possess similar characteristics). To achieve comparability, matching and randomization techniques should be used (Chapter 4). The experimental variable should be controlled, and it should be varied from one group to another. To test Hypothesis 1, the students in selected groups are given a formal questionnaire for evaluating the teacher's performance. The completed questionnaires are given to an authority figure who has higher prestige than does the teacher; for example, the authority figure might be the experimenter (who may be comparable to the dean in this situation). The teacher is then given direct feedback concerning the nature of the student evaluations. The teacher's rewards (money actually could be the reward) must be commensurate with the evaluations. It is not necessary to give the actual evaluations, but only to make the rewards and evaluations comparable.

To increase the variation in the experimental variable, in some groups, the students are simply not allowed to evaluate the teacher—that is, there is no formal technique such as utilization of a questionnaire; and in other groups, the students are allowed to fill out and turn in questionnaires, but the teacher is given rewards independent of their positive or negative evaluations.

In summary, there are three sets of groups in the experiment: (1) experimental group *A,* in which student evaluations are formally assessed and deemed important, (2) experimental group *B,* in which student evaluations are formally assessed but are not deemed important, and (3) the control group, in which student evaluations are not formally assessed. Hypothesis 1 will be supported if the teachers in the experimental groups use lower standards (are more lenient in grading) than do those in the control group. Moreover, teachers in the experimental group where student evaluations are formally assessed and deemed important should have the lowest standards of all.

methods of observation

Largely dependent upon the design (but also dependent upon the conceptual framework and the nature of the population and sample), observational techniques may take the form of a questionnaire, an interview (guide or schedule), physical devices, trace methods, or participant observation. If we had decided that very little is known about student evaluations and had selected a case-study design, then some form of participant observation would be most appropriate. We could play the role of the student, the teacher, the dean, or merely a nonmember classroom observer and, from our observations, try to formulate relevant concepts and hypotheses. A participant-observer may be aided in his observations by an interview guide, a tape recorder, a motion-picture camera, or an interaction-process analysis machine. To aid him in his analysis, he may keep a daily log of events.

An experiment or survey usually requires techniques other than participant observation. If a social survey is selected for the design (whether or not it is the cross-cultural, poll, or panel design), the questionnaire or interview is the most commonly chosen technique. If available, a few trace methods (accretion or erosion) may buttress the analysis.

Suppose a questionnaire is selected as the primary data source. The formulation of a questionnaire demands decisions in several areas. For example, should structured or unstructured items be used? This decision rests primarily on the degree of our confidence that we know the relevant alternatives to any particular question. For example, teacher attitudes toward student evaluations (if this information is necessary to the problem) may be far more complex than those allowed by the three response categories of "favorable," "neutral," or "unfavorable." Teachers may designate certain situations where such evaluations are relevant, while maintaining that students are not competent to make judgments about others. The decision-making process also must be applied to the questionnaire length, the wording of each individual question, and the use of transition statements. These problems by no means exhaust decision making; they only point to the complexity of the task and suggest the necessity of a high degree of skill and knowledge in formulating an adequate questionnaire.

Crucial to the formulation of the questionnaire are those particular items that comprise the operational definitions or indicators of the independent and dependent variables in the hypotheses. Consider the following, asked of students, teachers, and administrators, relating to the concepts in the three hypotheses about student evaluations:

1. STUDENT EVALUATIONS
   In your opinion, are student evaluations of teacher performance considered a major criterion by administrators in their evaluations of teachers?
   Yes____ No____

   In your opinion, how important are student evaluations in influencing a teacher's promotion and salary raises?
   ____very important
   ____somewhat important
   ____neither important nor unimportant
   ____relatively unimportant
   ____not considered at all

   How often do you think student evaluations are considered when a teacher's performance is evaluated?
   ____frequently
   ____sometimes
   ____rarely
   ____never

2. CLASSROOM STANDARDS
   Would you rate the overall grading standards in this college as easy____ or hard____?

   On the following scale, rate the teachers in the sociology department (or math department, etc.) on the severity of their grading standards:
   ____extremely hard
   ____hard
   ____neither hard nor easy

_____easy
_____extremely easy

3. MORALE
    Taking into consideration all the things about this
    college, how satisfied or dissatisfied are you with the
    way this college is run?
    _____very satisfied
    _____satisfied
    _____neither satisfied nor dissatisfied
    _____dissatisfied
    _____very dissatisfied

4. IDEAL EVALUATIONAL CRITERIA
    In your opinion, how important is teaching ability as
    a criterion for evaluating teachers?
    _____very important
    _____somewhat important
    _____neither important nor unimportant
    _____somewhat unimportant
    _____very unimportant

5. REAL EVALUATIONAL CRITERIA
    Is the ability to be a sympathetic listener a major
    criterion to evaluate a teacher?   Yes_____   No_____

    Is the style of dress a major criterion to evaluate a
    teacher?
    Yes_____   No_____

    In the evaluation of a teacher, how important is the
    ability to be a sympathetic listener?
    _____very important
    _____important
    _____neither important nor unimportant
    _____unimportant
    _____very unimportant

In the evaluation of a teacher, how important is style of dress?
____very important
____important
____neither important nor unimportant
____unimportant
____very unimportant

In the evaluation of a teacher, how important is the ability to be entertaining in class?
____very important
____important
____neither important nor unimportant
____unimportant
____very unimportant

In the evaluation of a teacher, how important is friendliness?
____very important
____important
____neither important nor unimportant
____unimportant
____very unimportant

6. THE TEACHER ROLE (for teachers only)
About how much time do you spend with students outside of the classroom per week?
____15 hours or more
____5 to 14 hours
____less than 5 hours

About how much time do you spend preparing lectures per week?
____20 hours or more
____10 to 19 hours
____less than 10 hours

About how many exams, on the average, do you
give in each course?

_____3 or more

_____2

_____1 or none

A few trace methods and secondary sources should be
used along with the questionnaire items to help evaluate the
validity of the questions and test the hypotheses. For example, a
student handbook or faculty manual (a secondary source) is
published yearly at many universities and colleges. These hand-
books often give a direct evaluation of teacher performance over
a period of time and in a variety of areas; e.g., they might
indicate whether the teacher's lectures are stimulating or boring,
the type of exams he gives, his class requirements, and his
grading standards. Such data could be used in testing Hypothesis 1, which requires information on a teacher's grading
standards over a period of time. The mere existence of the
handbook may influence teacher morale (and student morale)
and therefore lead to a test of Hypothesis 2. Furthermore, the
characteristics evaluated in the handbook indicate the stress on
ideal and real evaluational criteria.

Other secondary sources that may be useful are the
teacher absentee rate from class (as a measure of the teacher's
role or morale), the student absentee rate (as a measure of
morale), and the faculty turnover rate and their average length
of stay at the college (as a measure of morale).

A trace measure that may be used to evaluate time spent
in the teacher's role is the total number of pages of reading
material assigned to a class (less reading material may indicate
less preparation time). An example of an erosion-time measure
could be the number of students who drop a course, which may
indicate a negative evaluation of the teacher.

Unlike the survey, an experimental design may lend
itself to direct observational techniques by physical devices.
Consider the experiment set up under the research-design
section of this chapter. The experimenter may make direct

observations of the subjects (students and teachers) through a one-way mirror. He can directly observe both the teacher's performance and the reactions of students (without influencing the results by his presence). Although a questionnaire or exam can be used to evaluate a teacher's performance, an interaction-process analysis machine or chronograph may be used. One measure of the effectiveness of teaching could be the participation of students in discussions. The chronograph measures the degree of participation of each member, as well as indicating the initiators of interaction.

data analysis

Analysis of the data involves both descriptive and inference statistics. Descriptively, the data are summarized and reduced to a few meaningful statistics for the actual sample of students and teachers at each college and university studied. The descriptions pertain both to the nature of relevant characteristics of each institution and to the nature of the relations between the independent and dependent variables in the hypotheses. After these characteristics and relations have been established for the samples, inference statistics are used to make statements about the populations and the samples represented.

Among other characteristics, each sample should be described as to the nature of student evaluations, classroom standards, student and teacher morale, ideal and real evaluational criteria, and the various aspects of the teacher role. Average (mean, median, or modal) responses to questionnaire items should be reported, as well as some indication of the diversity of opinion (dispersion measures such as the standard deviation and average deviation). Perhaps frequency counts and percentage distributions for questionnaire items also should be reported. Most researchers would include a description of the individual institutions (private or public, size, location, college or university, etc.) and the composition of the student body (socioeconomic status, academic majors, sex ratio, GPAs, etc.). These characteristics, although not central to the testing of the hypotheses, provide a background for the assessment of the conditional nature of the findings. For example, the relation between student evaluations and low teacher morale may be relevant only for private colleges.

Finally, the relations between the hypothesized variables should be computed and described for each school. By the use of correlational statistics (for example, the correlation coefficient r or Spearman's rho), these relations can be reduced to a comprehensible summary measure. That is, a negative r or rho between the effectiveness of student evaluations and grading standards supports Hypothesis 1; a positive r or rho between the effectiveness of student evaluations and student morale supports Hypothesis 2. Also supporting Hypothesis 2 is a negative r or rho between the effectiveness of student evaluations and teacher morale. Finally, Hypothesis 3 is supported by a negative r or rho between the discrepancy of ideal and real criteria for evaluating teacher performance and time spent in the teacher role; that is, the higher the discrepancy, the less time spent in the teacher role.

Inference statistics are used to see if it is reasonable to generalize the above-mentioned univariate characteristics and bivariate relations of the sample to the population. A probability estimate may be made on each of the characteristics to establish a reasonable population range (for example, the GPA for the population may lie between 2.5 and 2.9 on a 4.0 scale). Tests of hypotheses may be applied to the r and rho correlations to see if it is reasonable to conclude that the observed relations in the sample hold for the total population. Population estimates also may be made for the relations. For example, the r between the effectiveness of student evaluations and grading standards in the population may lie between .40 and .60. Another frequently used inference technique is chi square, which may be applied to the relations between questionnaire items. A significant chi-square value indicates a non-zero relation between two items.

conclusions

The purpose of this chapter is twofold: (1) to summarize, by example, some of the major points stressed in the preceding chapters, and (2) to help you in setting up and carrying out sociological research. Treating scientific inquiry as a decision-making process, it is hoped, not only clarifies the research process, but provides a basis for insights into the problems encountered in doing social research.

Glossary

The meanings of the following terms are consistent with usage in this book.

accretion measure   Data based on the building up or the depositing of materials over a period of time, which is often gradual (refuse and remains of pottery).

adequacy of sample   The sample is of sufficient size to permit a specified confidence in inferences made to the population.

analysis of changes   Study of the differences in pairs of values at two or more time periods, such as individual scores in a pretest and posttest.

association   The statistical relation between two or more variables, either by covariation or joint occurrence.

average deviation   The mean or median differences (deviations) of all scores in a distribution. The absolute sum of all differences divided by the number of individuals.

behavioral equivalent   A measurable indicator of social phenomena; such as using attendance records as an indicator of group cohesion.

bivariate   Two variables, displayed in some relation to each other.

case study   The observation of one unit (population or sample) at one point in time.

cause see *scientific law*   A variable is considered a cause of another variable if it satisfies the criteria of (1) a non-zero association, (2) time priority, (3) nonspuriousness, and (4) rationale.

chi square   A statistical test indicating the probability that the observed distribution of two attributes or variables resulted from purely chance factors.

classical randomized experiment (CRE) or classical experimental design   A research design characterized by control over the experimental (independent) variable and comprised of both experimental and control groups.

concept   A symbol that represents the similarities in otherwise diverse phenomena.

consistency of association   A statistical relation that persists from one study to the next under a variety of conditions.

control, statistical   Manipulating a variable so that it does not influence the relation in question.

control group   Individuals in an experimental design that are observed but do not receive the experimental variable (stimulus).

correlation coefficient (r) A measure of relation based on the principle of covariation used with quantitative variables. One common interpretation is r^2, which refers to the amount of variance in one variable that is accounted for by the variation in another variable.

correlational study Comparison of two or more units at one point in time.

covariation For quantitative data, the situation where a unit change in one variable is paralleled with some degree of regularity by a comparable change in another variable; e.g., height and weight or education and income.

cross-classification A frequency distribution based on the simultaneous tabulation of the categories of two or more variables.

data reduction Grouping information into a few categories or computing a small number of statistics to adequately describe the characteristics of a sample or population.

definition A statement of intention to use a symbol in a specified way.

dependent variable The effect or variable that is caused by the independent variable; also, the variable that you are trying to explain.

depth interview Intensive questioning of respondents. In the social sciences this frequently refers to probing for the meaning of answers, usually in an unstructured situation.

description Statements about the characteristics of phenomena.

descriptive statistics Techniques and measures indicating the characteristics of the data at hand—for example, frequency distributions, typical values, dispersion, and relations.

dispersion (variation, spread, scatter) The amount of spread or differences among the scores of a distribution.

double blind   An experiment during which the true nature of the experimental variable is unknown to both subject and researcher.

empathy   General: A state of feeling with others. Specific: Understanding; associated with an approach in sociology called *Verstehen.* It is a type of exploration that stresses a similarity in emotional feeling between the scientist and the subject.

empirical   Subject to observation through sense perceptions.

enumeration   The counting of units, such as the number of persons in an area.

erosion measure   Data based on the wearing away, often gradual, of some material (shoe or tile wear).

error rate   The degree of risk taken (probability of error) in inferring the results of the sample to the population.

evidence, scientific   Empirical information used to evaluate the truth or falsity of a statement or hypothesis.

experimental group   The group in an experiment comprised of individuals or units receiving the experimental variable (stimulus).

experimental variable   The stimulus administered to the experimental group between pretest and posttest.

explanation, scientific   The subsuming of a fact or relation under a scientific law.

fact, scientific   Empirically validated and reliable information, according to the methods of science.

frequency distribution   The separation of a variable into mutually exclusive classes and the number of individuals in each class.

history   Extraneous events other than the experimental variable, occurring between pretest and posttest, that may affect the results of the study.

hypothesis   A statement of relation between two or more variables that is subject to empirical test.

independent variable   The causal or explanatory variable that
occurs, or is assumed to occur, prior to the dependent
variable.

indicator   An indirect measure of an abstract and general
variable. For example, a low suicide rate is an indicator
of a healthy society.

inference statistics   Techniques used to estimate population characteristics from sample data.

instrument decay   A state in which the measuring instrument in a
study loses its effectiveness; for example, springs on
scales may lose their tension, or long questionnaires may
cause fatigue or loss of interest.

interquartile range   Dispersion measure that gives the distance
(range) encompassing the middle 50 percent of the
scores in a distribution.

intervening mechanisms   Factors that are seen as occurring between and connecting the independent and dependent
variables.

interview   The situation in which answers are directly elicited
from subjects by a person who asks for and usually
records responses.

interview guide   An observational instrument comprised of a
series of unstructured questions or general topics that
are asked and filled in by an interviewer.

joint occurrence   In compiling qualitative data, the situation
where individuals can be placed in several categories
simultaneously—for example, "male" and "delinquent"
or "easy" and "professor."

judge   An observer who is detached from the situation and uses
a fairly rigid set of predetermined categories by which to
code events.

lambda   A measure of relation based on joint occurrence, which indicates the proportionate reduction in error by using a predictor variable over the original error that is based on choosing the largest marginal frequency in the dependent variable.

logical conclusion   A deduced statement from a premise that follows certain clearly specified rules.

longitudinal study   Observations of one unit over a period of time.

magnitude of association   Size of the relation between two or more variables.

matching   The selection of units or individuals into experimental and control groups on the basis of similar characteristics.

maturation   The changes in subjects (not produced by the experimental variable) by such factors as aging or learning that may affect the results of the study.

mean   The arithmetic average, which is the sum of all the scores divided by their number.

measurement   The assignment, according to rules, of numbers or other symbols to categories or classes.

median   The category or value above and below which 50 percent of the total frequency lies, or the middle category dividing the distribution into two equal parts.

mode   The category (or categories) containing the highest frequency in a frequency distribution.

mortality (design)   Subjects who, for any reason, do not complete a study; e.g., death, refusal, illness, or moving away.

multiple causation   A dependent variable is produced by two or more independent variables.

multiple r   The relation based on covariation between one dependent variable and two or more independent variables. It may be interpreted as the amount of variance in the dependent variable that is accounted for by an additive combination of the variation in the independent variables.

multistage areal sampling   The random selection of territorial units, proceeding from, first, a selection of large units, then to selection of smaller and smaller units.

multivariate analysis   The simultaneous analysis of three or more variables, either for the purpose of prediction or to control for selected factors.

natural setting   The everyday environment of persons being studied, as opposed to the contrived settings of most experiments.

necessary condition   A factor or variable that must be present before another factor or variable can occur, whether the other factor does or does not occur. A condition in whose absence the event cannot occur.

negative (inverse) relation   Two or more variables change in opposite directions: as one increases the other decreases.

nonspurious relation   A situation in which the relation between two or more variables cannot be explained by a third variable.

norming   Controlling for a third factor by including that factor in the actual values of a variable; e.g., percentages, proportions, ratios, and indexes.

operational definition   The steps in the measurement or observational procedures are clearly specified so that competent observers will come up with the same results when measuring the same phenomenon. The specification of the procedures that are necessary for identifying the concept in question.

panel design Repeated observations of the same sample or population over a period of time.

participant observation Observers take an active part in the situation they are studying in order to record .events. The researcher participates in his own study while gathering data on respondents.

physical-trace evidence Observational data based on erosion or accretion measures.

population (universe) The largest number of individuals or units of interest to the researcher.

positive (direct) relation Two or more variables change in the same direction: that is, as one increases, the other increases.

posttest Observations made after the experimental variable (stimulus) has been administered.

prediction A statement about the expected values of a variable not yet observed that is based on the knowledge of the values of another variable. Sometimes used to refer to a quantitative statement concerning a relation between two or more variables.

predictive ability The degree to which one can use the values of one variable to estimate accurately the values of another variable.

pretest Observations made prior to the experimental variable (stimulus).

primary data Information gathered and used by the researcher.

probability, statistical The relative frequency with which an event occurs or is likely to occur.

qualitative Distinguishing one class of objects from another by type or kind rather than by magnitude, as for example, in distinguishing males from females.

quantitative Measurement of variables in terms of magnitude, extent, or amount, such as height, weight, and population size.

questionnaire An observational instrument comprised of a series of questions that are answered by the respondent himself.

quota sample A nonrandom procedure where the population is stratified and a percentage of each stratum is selected. The final selection of cases is left to the interviewer.

random sample, simple Each individual has an equal chance of being chosen, and the selection of any one individual has no effect on the selection of any other.

randomization A process by which subjects are assigned to experimental and control groups on a probabilistic basis for the purpose of equating the two groups on all known and unknown characteristics.

range, total The highest minus the lowest scores in a distribution.

ranking Establishing classes of a variable into greater than or less than other classes on a selected dimension; for example, on prestige, professional occupations are ranked higher than manual occupations.

rationale Statements logically justifying the relation between two or more variables.

reactive measure An observational instrument that sensitizes respondents to certain events. It often results in bias by changing the subjects' responses.

regression, statistical The tendency of extreme scores to be less extreme in a subsequent period of observation; they regress toward the mean.

reliability The condition in which repeated observations of the same phenomena with the same instrument yield similar results.

representativeness of sample The degree to which the sample reflects the characteristics of the population.

research design Selection of units and comparative forms to make descriptive statements or test hypotheses.

research problem The ideas to be assessed in a study; usually refers to the first step in the scientific method.

rho A measure of relation usually applied to rank-order data and referring to the degree of agreement between two rank orders.

sample A part of a population.

sampling bias The degree to which the sample does not reflect the characteristics of the population.

sampling error Unrepresentativeness due to random fluctuations.

schedule, interview An observational instrument comprised of a series of questions that are asked and filled in by an interviewer in a face-to-face situation with the respondent.

science Any discipline in which theory is validated through empirical observations.

scientific (causal) law A hypothesis that has been repeatedly supported by empirical tests (which satisfy the criteria of a non-zero association, time priority of the independent variable, nonspuriousness, and rationale).

scientific method A procedure for discovering the conditions under which specified events occur, generally characterized by tentativeness, verifiability, rigorous reasoning, and empirical observation.

scientific theory A set of interrelated propositions that comprise a deductive system.

secondary data   Information that is not collected by the investigator but is used by him, such as census reports and company records.

selection   A process by which individuals are placed into groups. A self-selection bias often results if the researcher cannot use randomization or matching to equate the groups.

sensitization   The process of making subjects aware of factors in the study that changes their responses.

social survey   A design usually involving a rather large sample of a population or some one selected segment; it is usually associated with the observational techniques of the questionnaire and interview.

spatial control   Achievement, by matching and randomization, of pretest equality between experimental and control groups.

standard deviation   The square root of the averaged squared differences (deviations) from the mean of a distribution.

standard unit   An established dimension by which units are measured, such as the foot, the hour, or the pound.

standardization   Controlling for the effects of a third factor by adjusting the data to one or more characteristics of a constant (standard) distribution.

structured question   Statements that have a limited number of explicit responses from which the respondent can choose.

subclassification (partialling)   A procedure for control by computing separate measures of relation for each category of a third variable that is affecting the relation in question.

sufficient condition   The presence of one factor always leads to the presence of another specified factor.

table An ordered arrangement of numerical data placed in rows and columns, with concise labels specifying the nature of the data.

temporal control Elimination of the effects of extraneous factors occurring between the pretest and posttest by use of a control group.

10th–90th percentile range Dispersion measure giving the distance (range) encompassing the middle 80 percent of the scores in a distribution.

time priority One variable occurs first or changes prior to another variable.

typical value (central tendency) The average score or most frequently counted category of a variable; for example, the median, the mean, or the mode.

univariate A single variable.

unstructured question Open-ended statements to which the respondent gives his own answer.

validity The soundness of the theoretically defined meaning of a variable, i.e., a valid measure, or of the true relation between variables, i.e., a valid relationship. A valid technique measures what it is supposed to measure. A valid relationship is based on valid measures, unbiased research designs, and representative samples.

variable A measurable dimension of a concept that takes on two or more values.

yule's Q A measure of relation based on joint occurrence applicable only to the two-by-two table.

Index